Assessing and Treating Culturally Diverse Clients

Second Edition

MULTICULTURAL ASPECTS OF COUNSELING SERIES

SERIES EDITOR

Paul Pedersen, Ph.D., *University of Alabama at Birmingham*

EDITORIAL BOARD

VOLUMES IN THIS SERIES

Assessing and Treating Culturally Diverse Clients

A Practical Guide
Second Edition

Freddy A. Paniagua

Multicultural Aspects of Counseling Series 4

SAGE Publications
International Educational and Professional Publisher
Thousand Oaks   London   New Delhi

For information:

 SAGE Publications, Inc.
2455 Teller Road
Thousand Oaks, California 91320
E-mail: order@sagepub.com

SAGE Publications Ltd.
6 Bonhill Street
London EC2A 4PU
United Kingdom

SAGE Publications India Pvt. Ltd.
M-32 Market
Greater Kailash I
New Delhi 110 048 India

Printed in the United States of America

Library of Congress Cataloging-in-Publication Data

Main entry under title:

Paniagua, Freddy A.
    Assessing and treating culturally diverse clients : a practical guide / by Freddy A. Paniagua. — 2nd ed.
        p. cm. — (Multicultural aspects of counseling : vol. 4)
    Includes bibliographical references and index.
        ISBN 0-7619-1049-2 (alk. paper). — ISBN 0-7619-1050-6 (pbk.: alk. paper)
        1. Cross-cultural counseling—United States. I. Title.
    II. Series: Multicultural aspects of counseling : v. 4.
    BF637.C6P264 1998
    361'.06'089—dc21   97-45260

98 99 00 01 02 03   10 9 8 7 6 5 4 3 2

Acquiring Editor:	Jim Nageotte
Editorial Assistant:	Fiona Lyon
Production Editor:	Michele Lingre
Production Assistant:	Lynn Miyata
Typesetter/Designer:	Danielle Dillahunt
Print Buyer:	Anna Chin

Contents

Series Editor's Introduction

The high demand for practical guidelines to assess and treat culturally diverse clients is reflected in the popularity of the first edition of Dr. Paniagua's book. This second edition builds on the popularity of the first edition. As providers become more aware of the importance of cultural diversity, the demand for practical guidelines has rapidly increased. This second edition is in response to that demand.

The research literature on multicultural counseling has been increasing so rapidly that surveys of literature more than 5 years in print are at a severe disadvantage. Dr. Paniagua has carefully brought up to date the chapters on guidelines for assessment and treatment of the different American ethnic groups. New ideas for prevention, evaluation, and epidemiological mental health methodologies have also been included to supplement materials in the first edition.

As in the first edition, the practical focus of Dr. Paniagua's book builds on several assumptions. First, tests and measures developed in one cultural context will reflect elements of that cultural context bias when used in a different and contrasting cultural context. All tests and measures are therefore to some extent culturally biased. Second, it is possible for a skilled provider to accurately, meaningfully, and appropriately interpret data from biased assessments and measures to culturally different consumers. Third, Dr. Paniagua's book provides the practical guidelines needed for accurate, meaningful, and appropriate interpretation of data from culturally biased measures and assessments.

Chapter 10, new to this edition, on the interpretation of the American Psychiatric Association's *DSM-IV* (1994), is particularly valuable, dealing with cultural variations across all disorders. Dr. Paniagua carefully documents the literature to create new sets of tables for matching *DSM-IV* disorders with cultural variables. This alternative interpretation of *DSM-IV* categories has been pretested among residents in psychiatry, postdoctoral fellows in psychology, and social workers, who found the chapter useful in locating cultural variables in the *DSM-IV*. This chapter will be particularly useful for clinicians to rapidly screen for cultural variables.

Dr. Paniagua has incorporated feedback from readers of the first edition to update demographic information across groups, enlarge the index, modify the terminology, and incorporate new research studies. As with the first edition, the primary benefit of this second edition will be in offering a practical approach for assessing and treating culturally different groups and a quick review of the major points clinicians should know when serving these groups.

Dr. Paniagua's book makes an important and significant contribution to the *Multicultural Aspects of Counseling* (MAC) series. This book models the practical emphasis demonstrated by each of the MAC books published.

—Paul Pedersen

Preface

Why This Book Was Written

Four major multicultural groups in mental health practices are African Americans, American Indians, Asians, and Hispanics. A major task for practitioners across all mental health disciplines (psychology, psychiatry, social work, family therapy, and the like) is to learn and apply skills that indicate that they are culturally competent in the assessment and treatment of clients from these groups (Pope-Davis & Coleman, 1997). Relevant questions in the assessment and treatment of multicultural groups include the following:

- What should a practitioner do during the first meeting or session with an African American client versus an Asian client?
- Would a practitioner treat an American Indian client with the same therapeutic approach as a Hispanic client?
- What exactly would a practitioner do to assess or treat these groups differently?
- What are some examples of cross-cultural skills a practitioner should display to minimize biases when assessing clients from different multicultural groups?

These questions are not only clinically relevant, but also a failure to answer them and to demonstrate their use in clinical practices may be considered as an example of lacking cultural competence and a violation of ethical principles (LaFromboise, Foster, & James, 1996). For example, in the new code of ethics from the American Psychological Association (APA, 1992), mental health professionals "must be aware of cultural, individual, and role differences, including those due to age, gender, *race, ethnicity, national origin, religion . . . language,* and *socioeconomic status* [italics added]" (pp. 3-4). A violation of this principle would be considered a case of "unfair discriminatory practices" (APA, 1992, p. 3). In addition, the written and oral exams required for licensure in the practice of psychologists, psychiatrists, social workers, and other mental health professionals include items dealing with the under-standing and application of cultural variables that might affect the assess-ment and treatment of multicultural groups seeking mental health services.

An excellent literature is available to help mental health practitioners in the development and application of cross-cultural skills in their clinical contacts with these multicultural groups (Bamford, 1991; Berry, Poortinga, Segall, & Darsen, 1992; Comas-Díaz & Griffith, 1988; Dana, 1993b; Gaw, 1993a; Ho, 1992; Koslow & Slett, 1989; Lefley & Pedersen, 1986; McAdoo, 1993; Pedersen, 1987, 1997; Ponterotto, Casas, Suzuki, & Alexander, 1995; Seijo, Gomez, & Freidenberg, 1991; Sue & Sue, 1990; Tharp, 1991). Prac-tical guidelines in the assessment and treatment of these groups, however, are either dispersed across the literature (e.g., Comas-Díaz, 1988; Dana, 1993b; Koslow & Slett, 1989) or mixed with discussions of philosophical, political, and theoretical issues regarding the assessment and treatment of such groups (e.g., Berry et al., 1992; Sue & Sue, 1990). Practitioners interested in self-training regarding cultural competence in the assessment and treatment of multicultural groups lack an integrative approach in which such guidelines are summarized in a single text.

In addition, discussion of multicultural issues in mental health (particu-larly in the areas of treatment and assessment) is evolving rapidly; practitio-ners may be having a difficult time keeping up with this movement while engaging in their routine clinical practices. The main goal of *Assessing and Treating Culturally Diverse Clients* is to provide an integrative and practical answer to the following question: What exactly should a mental health practitioner do or not do to demonstrate cultural competence and avoid unfair discriminatory practices during the assessment and treatment of African American, American Indian, Asian, and Hispanic clients?

Overview

It is important to emphasize that descriptions of cultural variables in this book reflect generalizations that may not be true for all members of a group or for each subgroup in a given group (e.g., in the case of Hispanics, the subgroup of Cubans vs. the subgroup of Mexican Americans). As noted by Sue and Sue (1990), it is erroneous to believe that all African Americans are the same, that all Hispanics are the same, that all Asians are the same, or that all American Indians are the same. Differences across these groups and subgroups exist in terms of primary language (particularly among the Asians), generational status (e.g., early vs. later immigrants), acculturation, and socioeconomic status (Sue & Sue, 1987, 1990). These groups and subgroups, however, do share some cultural variables often considered as relevant in the assessment and treatment of all multicultural groups, regardless of group identity (e.g., all groups and subgroups prefer family relationships emphasizing the extended family rather than the nuclear family). This sharing of cultural variables across diverse groups and subgroups might be termed *cultural commonalities* (a term adopted from Chung, 1992).

The main purpose of *Assessing and Treating Culturally Diverse Clients* is to provide a summary of examples of cultural commonalities across groups (Chapters 2 and 7-9) and within subgroups (Chapters 3-6) that clinicians can use to guide their clinical practices with African American, Hispanic, Asian, and American Indian clients.

The book is composed of the original nine chapters and a new chapter (Chapter 10). Chapter 1 proposes a tentative explanation for the growing use of the terms *multicultural* or *diversity* and less emphasis on the term minority in the literature. This chapter also includes a brief discussion on the distinction between the terms *race* and *ethnicity*.

Chapter 2 presents an overview of general guidelines regarding the development of a therapeutic relationship that seems relevant to the four culturally diverse groups included in this text. In Chapters 3 through 6, in addition to an overview of demographic characteristics, three sets of practical guidelines are described for African American (Chapter 3), Hispanic (Chapter 4), Asian (Chapter 5), and American Indian clients (Chapter 6): guidelines on cultural variables that may affect assessment and treatment, guidelines for the session, and guidelines for conducting psychotherapy. Chapter 7 presents a summary of practical guidelines for understanding and preventing attrition among the target multicultural groups. Chapter 8 is an attempt to assist practitioners in the critical review and evaluation of epidemiological studies dealing with the prevalence and incidence of mental disorders among the four multicultural groups.

Chapter 9 makes an obvious point: Most measures or assessments used by practitioners today with African American, American Indian, Asian, and Hispanic clients are culturally biased. Because of practical and economical reasons, however, it may not be advisable to recommend that practitioners should not use these measures or assessments. A better alternative would be to train practitioners to use culturally biased measures. Practitioners need to know how to recognize such biases and how to accommodate data accurately and appropriately to be meaningful and helpful with culturally diverse clients.

The newest edition of the *Diagnostic and Statistical Manual of Mental Disorders* (*DSM-IV*; American Psychiatric Association, 1994) made a major contribution in terms of the inclusion of specific cultural variables across most psychiatric disorders. The *DSM-IV* strongly encourages practitioners to use these variables during the assessment and diagnosis of such disorders. These cultural variables, however, are dispersed across the *DSM-IV,* and they are not recommended across all psychiatric disorders. Chapter 10 summarizes these variables, and the chapter tables provide practitioners with a rapid screening of these variables.

Acknowledgments

I am indebted to many people whose support and advice played a major role in the preparation of this book. I thank F. M. Baker (University of Maryland) and Sharon Nelson Le-Gall (University of Pittsburgh) for their review of Chapter 3 (African Americans) and valuable suggestions. Richard H. Dana (Portland State University) reviewed the guidelines involving the use of the epidemiology of mental health literature with multicultural groups (Chapter 8) and the guidelines concerning the use of culturally biased instruments (Chapter 9). He sent me an extensive commentary regarding ways to improve these chapters, and I am grateful to him for his comments. Derald W. Sue (California State University at Hayward) and Anh Nga Nguyen (University of Oklahoma Health Sciences Center) assisted with Chapter 5 (Asians), and I also thank them for their comments. D. W. Sue also reviewed Chapter 2 (general guidelines); I particularly thank him for updating the references on Asian Americans. I thank Stanley Sue (University of California at Los Angeles) for reviewing portions of Chapters 1 and 2, particularly in relation to the discussion on cultural mismatch and racial mismatch.

Arthur McDonald (President, Dull Knife Memorial College, Lame Deer, MT) reviewed the chapter on American Indian clients, and I thank him for making me aware of several sensitive issues in the assessment and treatment of American Indian clients. Lillian Comas-Díaz (independent practice, Washington, D.C.) made substantial revisions regarding guidelines in the assessment and treatment of Hispanic clients (Chapter 4), including translation of terms from English to Spanish, a better interpretation of the acknowledgment of spiritual issues by Hispanic clients during the first session, and the enhancement of the references dealing with the assessment and treatment of Hispanic clients. I thank her for her effort and time in revising these materials.

Sylvia Z. Ramirez (University of Texas at Austin) and Sylvia Linares were clinical fellows under my supervision at the time I was organizing my thoughts to write this book. I discussed many of the topics in this text with them, and I thank them for their suggestions. I also thank Sylvia Ramirez for reviewing Chapters 4 and 8 and for her suggestion to include additional cultural variables, leading to a better understanding in the assessment and treatment of Hispanic clients. Victor L. Tan and Angela S. Lew were clinical fellows under my supervision at the time I wrote Chapter 10, and I thank them for their comments and suggestions for improving this chapter.

I have spent many hours during the past 5 years discussing cross-cultural issues with Israel Cuellar (University of Texas-Pan American University at Edinburg). He was the first person (as far as I can remember) who encouraged me to write this book. He reviewed Chapters 4, 8, and 9. I thank him deeply for his comments and suggestions on how to improve these chapters.

I thank Paul Pedersen, Series Editor, who was instrumental in the final preparation of this book for publication. He spent many hours reading each chapter and making sure that the book reflects practical guidelines for clinicians interested in the assessment and treatment of multicultural groups and that the book contains minimal rhetoric about multiculturalism.

I also thank the staff of Sage Publications for their time and effort in the preparation of the book. I particularly thank Ms. Marquita Flemming and Ms. Dale Mary Grenfell for their assistance and technical advice.

Book reviews have been very encouraging, and their critiques have been used to correct several points in this edition. I also thank the reviewers for their comments. Several readers have taken the time to send me letters clarifying issues that I have also integrated in this edition; I thank these readers for their letters of encouragement.

I especially thank my spouse, Sandra A. Black (Sam), and my son, Robert Alexander Paniagua (Rap), for their support and patience throughout the duration of this book.

Finally, it is important to recognize that this topic is extremely sensitive, and that I am responsible for any error or misunderstanding the reader may find in the text. I deeply appreciate comments or suggestions from readers for consideration in future editions of this book. Please send your comments to Sage Publications, 2455 Teller Road, Thousand Oaks, CA 91320.

1

Minority, Multicultural, Race, and Ethnicity Concepts

Minority Groups Versus Multicultural Groups

In general, the term *minority* represents both a number and disadvantages in terms of socioeconomic status (Ho, 1987, 1992; Sue & Sue, 1990; Wilkinson, 1993). Thus, in the United States, Anglo-Americans or whites are not considered a "minority group" because there are too many of them (approximately 215-221 million in 1995), and their socioeconomic status is often higher than that of other groups (U.S. Bureau of the Census, 1996). African Americans, however, are considered a minority group because they number approximately 33.6 million (U.S. Bureau of the Census, 1996) and their socioeconomic status is considered lower than that of the "majority" (i.e., whites). Other examples of minority groups in terms of their number and socioeconomic status in 1995 (U.S. Bureau of the Census, 1996), include American Indians, Asians and Pacific Islanders, and Hispanics. The term minority, however, may not be appropriate for three reasons: discrepancy in income level across minority groups, the impact of minority groups on other groups, and the implication that the term minority is another term for "inferiority" in the minds of some members of such groups.

1

Discrepancy in Income
Levels Across Minority Groups

When comparing median income levels across minority groups (e.g., Asians vs. African Americans), one finds a discrepancy. For example, in 1995, the median income for the Asian and Pacific Islander population (e.g., Japanese, Chinese, Filipino, and Hawaiian) was $46,106, and the median income for African Americans in the same year was $24,698; the national U.S. median income was $39,276 (U.S. Bureau of the Census, 1996). Asians, Pacific Islanders, and African Americans are examples of minority groups in the United States in terms of their number (and in comparison with the Anglo-Americans). In 1995, however, the Asian and Pacific Islander population reported a median income far above the national average.

A similar point could be made when income levels across subgroups within the same ethnic group are compared. For example, the median income for the Cubans (a subgroup of Hispanics) in 1995 was $30,584, whereas the median income for Puerto Ricans (another subgroup of Hispanics) was $20,929. In addition, in 1995, the income levels of 33.2% of Puerto Rican families and 36% of Puerto Ricans (persons) were below the poverty level in comparison with only 13.6% (families) and 17.8% (persons) reported by the Cubans (U.S. Bureau of the Census, 1996). Cubans and Puerto Ricans are examples of minority groups in the United States, but it is evident that the Cubans have a higher standard of living in the United States than the Puerto Ricans do.

Therefore, although a person could be considered by others as a minority because that person is a member of a small number of people in comparison with the majority, that person may not share the same minority status when income level is considered (either between minority groups or between subgroups within the same racial group).

Impact of Minority
Groups on Other Groups

Another problem with the use of the term minority is that it does not take into consideration the influence of the population size of a minority group on another minority group (Wilkinson, 1986). For example, many African Americans and Hispanics reside in Florida. A major problem confronting the African Americans, however, is that in several sections of Florida (e.g., Miami), they constitute a minority group, whereas the Hispanics constitute a majority group. Both groups are examples of minority populations when the number of people in the United States is considered in the definition of minority. In such sections of Florida, however, the African Americans are the minority and the Hispanics constitute the majority. A similar comparison could be made in the case of the population of the Lower Rio Grande Valley of Texas (which is concentrated along the U.S.-Mexican border). In this region, the Mexican Americans are the majority; other Hispanics (e.g., Puerto Ricans and Cubans), Asians, African Americans, and American Indians are minority groups.

The Concept of Minority
as a Case for Inferiority

Practitioners should be aware that some people do not want to be called minority because this term implies inferiority and a sense of superiority by those in the majority (i.e., Anglo-Americans). For example, in a letter sent to the *San Antonio Express News,* a Hispanic wrote, "When an individual labels me a 'minority,' I feel small, weak, and irrelevant. On the other hand, 'ethnically diverse American' is empowering and more accurate" (R. E. Martinez, 1993, p. 5B). Furthermore, McAdoo (1993a) pointed out that a major reason to avoid the term minority is that "it has an insidious implication of *inferiority* [italics added]. . . . A sense of superiority is assumed by those of the implied superior status" (p. 6).

Thus, it seems that the term minority may not be applicable when issues involving income level, the impact of minority groups on other minority groups, and the potential use of the term as synonymous with inferiority are considered (Kim, McLeod, & Shantzis, 1992; McAdoo, 1993b; Wilkinson, 1986). Perhaps more appropriate terms would include multicultural and diversity populations or groups. These terms emphasize the fact that two groups may be among the few in terms of their number in the United States, but the same groups are different in terms of cultural values. The use of these concepts (instead of the concept minority group) is gradually appearing in the literature (e.g., Dana, 1993b).

In the assessment and treatment of people with mental disorders, a practical guideline is to emphasize the ways different multicultural groups express their cultural values, their view about the world, and their place in society rather than an emphasis on the minority group per se. For example, African Americans and Anglo-Americans are examples of multicultural groups in the United States. Other multicultural groups seen with less frequency in mental health services in the United States include the Greek, Italian, Irish, and Polish Americans and the West Indian Islanders (Allen,

1988; Jalali, 1988). This book summarizes practical guidelines in the assessment and treatment of four multicultural groups often seen in mental health services: African Americans, American Indians, Asians, and Hispanics.

Race Versus Ethnicity

A controversy exists regarding the interchangeable use of the terms race and ethnicity (Phinney, 1996). Both terms seem to label two different processes (Berry et al., 1992; Betancourt & Lopez, 1993; Garza-Treviño, Ruiz, & Venegas-Samuels, 1997; Wilkinson, 1993). An understanding of these processes is an important factor in the assessment and treatment of multicultural groups. As noted by Wilkinson (1993), *race* "is a category of persons who are related by a common heredity or ancestry and who are perceived and responded to in terms of external features or traits" (p. 19). *Ethnicity,* however, often refers to "a shared culture and lifestyles" (Wilkinson, 1993, p. 19). An individual could belong to a particular race without sharing ethnic identity with that race. For example, the fact that two Hispanic clients share a common heredity or ancestry does not necessarily mean that they also share the same ethnic identity (e.g., culture, values, lifestyles, beliefs, and norms). This difference in ethnic identity could be explained in terms of the process of acculturation (see Chapter 2), which may have a tremendous implication in the assessment and treatment of many diverse groups. Thus, an important guideline is not to assume that, because two clients share the same racial group, they also share the same ethnicity (e.g., values and lifestyles).

2

General Guidelines for the Assessment and Treatment of Multicultural Groups

This chapter summarizes general guidelines that are recommended in the literature (e.g., Dana, 1993b; Ho, 1987, 1992; Ivey, Ivey, & Simek-Morgan, 1996; Pedersen, 1997; Pedersen, Draguns, Lonner, & Trimble, 1996; Ponderotto, Casas, Suzuki, & Alexander, 1995) for all multicultural groups discussed in this book.

Development of a
Therapeutic Relationship

The therapeutic relationship seems paramount with all multicultural groups (Ho, 1992; Sue & Sue, 1990). In general, the development of this relationship involves three levels.

The *conceptual* level could include the client's and therapist's perception of sincerity, openness, honesty, motivation, empathy, sensitivity, inquiring concerns, and credibility. The *behavioral* level may include the client's perception of a therapist as competent in his or her profession, which may include issues regarding the training of the therapist as well as evidence of the specialization in the assessment and treatment of particular mental health problems (e.g., expertise in the assessment and treatment of depression). The behavioral level also reflects the therapist's perception of his or her clients as competent in terms of the clients' ability to follow direction and to use skills to self-implement the treatment plan as discussed between the therapist and the clients.

The *cultural* level generally includes two hypotheses (Lonner & Ibrahim, 1996; Paniagua, 1996; Paniagua, Wassef, O'Boyle, Linares, & Cuellar, 1993; Tharp, 1991). The *cultural compatibility hypothesis* suggests that the assessment and treatment of multicultural groups would be enhanced if racial and ethnic barriers between the client and the therapist are minimized. As these racial and ethnic differences between the client and the therapist approach zero, the therapist is effective in terms of providing both cultural and sensitive assessment and treatment to a particular group (Dana, 1993b; Lopez, Lopez, & Fong, 1991; Paniagua, 1996; Sue & Sue, 1990; Sue & Sundberg, 1996). For example, this hypothesis suggests that the assessment and treatment of an African American client would be enhanced if the therapist is also an African American. The racial and ethnic similarity in turn reinforces the client-therapist therapeutic relationship.

The cultural compatibility hypothesis, however, may not be practical in clinical practices for several reasons. First, in a test of this hypothesis, Sue, Fujino, Hu, Takeuchi, and Zane (1991) found that racial "match failed to be a significant predictor of treatment outcome, except for Mexican Americans" (p. 539). The other groups in this study were Asian American, African American, and white. These authors also found that racial match "appears to have a much greater impact on length of treatment [defined as dropping out and number of sessions] than on outcome" (p. 539).

Many members of culturally diverse groups (particularly African Americans) have been part of outcome research conducted by white investigators; the overall conclusion is that the race or ethnicity of the investigator had no effect on outcome (Sue, 1988). This point is particularly evident in the case of behavioral approaches (including behavior analysis, behavior therapy, and cognitive-behavioral modification; Paniagua & Baer, 1981), which are currently the dominant approaches used by white investigators and clinicians. Many research subjects included in these approaches have been selected from a wide range of culturally diverse groups; the results clearly show the effectiveness of such approaches in the treatment of clients from any race or ethnic background (e.g., Kolko, 1987). In fact, it is widely believed by culturally diverse clinicians and investigators that behavioral approaches are probably the most effective strategies in the assessment and treatment of the multicultural groups discussed in this book (Boyd-Franklin, 1989; Walker & LaDue, 1986; Yamamoto, Silva, Justice, Chang, & Leong, 1993). This is because these strategies are authoritative, concrete, action oriented, and emphasize immediate-focused learning factors generally preferred by these groups (Boyd-Franklin, 1989; Walker & LaDue, 1986).

Sue (1988) advises that racial match may lead to cultural mismatch, but racial "mismatches do not necessarily imply cultural mismatches, because therapists and clients from different [racial] groups may share similar values, lifestyles, and experiences" (p. 306). That is, in terms of the distinction between race and ethnicity discussed in Chapter 1, the therapist and the client may share the same racial group (e.g., both Hispanics), but they may not share the same ethnicity (e.g., they have different values and lifestyles). For example, highly acculturated Hispanic therapists working with less acculturated Hispanic clients may result in cultural mismatching (e.g., the therapist and the client do not share similar lifestyles and values), regardless of the fact that both therapist and client share the same racial group. Similarly, white therapists working with highly acculturated Hispanic clients may result in cultural matches (e.g., both share Western culture, values, and traditions), regardless of the racial mismatch.

Because of a history of hostile relations among some Asian nations (e.g., wars between Chinese and Japanese, Japanese and Korean, and Chinese and Vietnamese), it may not be practical to recommend the applicability of the cultural compatibility hypothesis with these groups (Yamamoto, 1993). If an older Japanese client is assigned for assessment and evaluation to a Chinese therapist, this relationship may create tension and mistrust, leading to potential failures in the treatment of the client. Thus, before an Asian therapist is recommended in the assessment and treatment of Asian clients, it may be appropriate to explore the potential impact of historical events.

Because of these problems with the cultural compatibility hypothesis, a second hypothesis has been proposed. This alternative hypothesis is known as the *universalistic argument* (Dana, 1993b; Paniagua, 1996; Tharp, 1991). In this argument, effective assessment and treatment will be the same across all multicultural groups independent of the issue of client-therapist racial and ethnic differences or similarities. This hypothesis probably explains the current emphasis on the training of Anglo-American therapists in the assessment and treatment of the four major multicultural groups discussed in this book. This hypothesis (Atkinson & Wampold, 1993, p. 247; Baker, 1988, p. 157) proposes that what is relevant in the assessment and treatment of multicultural groups is evidence that the therapist can display both cultural sensitivity (i.e., awareness of cultural variables that may affect assessment and treatment) and *cultural competence* (i.e., translation of this awareness into behaviors leading to effective assessment and treatment of the particular multicultural group; see Atkinson & Wampold, 1993, p. 247; Baker, 1988, p. 157). Thus, in terms of this hypothesis, white therapists are as effective as African American therapists in the assessment and treatment of African American clients as long as these two qualities (sensitivity and competence) are manifested in the clinical practice of white therapists working with African American clients. The hypothesis also suggests that the fact that a therapist and his or her client share the same race and ethnicity (e.g., Hispanic therapist and clients sharing similar values and lifestyles) does not guarantee the effectiveness of assessment and treatment of the client; the therapist must also show evidence of sensitivity and competency to enhance the effectiveness of assessment and treatment strategies, regardless of the shared race and ethnicity dimension in the therapist-client relationship.

Two additional issues in the universalistic hypothesis are the concepts of credibility and giving (Sue & Sue, 1990; Sue & Sundberg, 1996; Sue & Zane, 1987). *Credibility* is the client's perception that the therapist is effective and trustworthy; *giving* deals with the client's recognition that the therapist has provided something of value in the client-therapist relationship. In summary, the alternative hypothesis states that the ability to communicate credibility in a giving, culturally sensitivity manner and to exhibit cultural competency during the assessment and treatment of multicultural groups is more important than the similarity in the therapist's and client's racial membership (Baker, 1988; Tharp, 1991).

The following sections discuss how practitioners from any racial group (including Anglos) can enhance or develop cultural sensitivity and competency in the assessment and treatment of African American, American Indian, Asian, and Hispanic clients, regardless of racial and ethnic differences or similarities between practitioners and their clients.

Acculturation

Acculturation is a variable that must be considered during the assessment and treatment of the four multicultural groups discussed in this book (Dana, 1993b; Ho, 1992). In general, acculturation may be defined in terms of the degree of integration of new cultural patterns into the original cultural patterns (Dana, 1993b; Grieger & Ponterotto, 1995; Moyerman & Forman, 1992). The process of acculturation can be internal and external.

In the internal process of acculturation, changes in cultural patterns may occur when a diverse group moves from one U.S. region to another (e.g., from one city to another within the same state or across states). For example, when American Indians living in Arizona or New Mexico (or other states with a large number of reservations) move from their reservations to cities, they experience the impact of a societal lifestyle quite different from their societal lifestyle experienced on the reservations. Competition and individualism are two values with little relevance among American Indians who reside on reservations. These values, however, are extremely important for anyone who resides outside a reservation. In this example, the group simply moves from one area to another within the United States; the assimilation of new values and lifestyles in the new area is a function of the process of internal acculturation. The impact of the internal process of acculturation would be minimal if an American Indian were to move from one reservation to another in the United States.

The internal process of acculturation is further illustrated by Hispanics residing in certain areas of New York City who move to certain areas in Florida (e.g., Miami). The impact of acculturation as an internal process would be minimal in comparison to a move from New York City to another city such as Lawrence, Kansas, with few shared cultural patterns between the Hispanics and residents. Another example is Mexican Americans who reside on the U.S.-Mexican border (particularly in the Lower Rio Grande Valley of Texas, including Edinburg, Brownsville, McCallen, and Harlingen). Mexican Americans who move from this region to another region that has few Mexican American cultural patterns (e.g., Washington, D.C.) would experience a difficult internal acculturation process. Mexican Americans who move from the U.S.-Mexican border into San Antonio, Texas, however, would not experience the internal process of acculturation (or its impact would be minimal) because many Mexican Americans residing on the U.S.-Mexican border and Mexicans Americans residing in San Antonio share similar cultural patterns.

In the external process of acculturation, a person moves from his or her country of origin to another country. This process is experienced by the Hispanics and Asians who move to the United States. The effects of the external acculturation process are less dramatic when immigrants move into the United States and reside in cities that resemble the norms, cultural patterns, and values of their home cities. This is the case for most Hispanics from Cuba, the Dominican Republic, and Puerto Rico residing in New York City and Miami as well as for Mexicans who move to U.S. cities located on the U.S. Mexican border. Hispanics residing in such U.S. cities not only encounter people who can understand their language but also find people from their countries of origin who share many of their cultural values (e.g., folk beliefs, customs, and music). The effect of the external acculturation process is more dramatic for those people who move to the United States and reside in a city in which there is little similarity to their original cultural patterns.

Levels of Acculturation

It is important to determine the potential impact of different levels of acculturation on the assessment and treatment of a client. These levels can be defined in terms of number of years in the internal or the external acculturation process, age at which the client enters such a process, and country of origin. The general assumption is that younger clients are more easily acculturated than older clients, and that as the number of years in the process increases, the level of acculturation also increases. In terms of the country of origin, the main assumption is that a racial group tends to show a higher level of acculturation depending on its country of origin. For example, a client from the Dominican Republic residing in New York City is more easily acculturated than a client from Vietnam residing in the same city because the Dominican experienced (in his or her country of origin) many U.S. cultural values prior to entering the United States, including dress style, music, language (many Dominicans speak English prior to entering the United States), and a competitive approach.

Chapter 8 (Table 8.1) provides examples of acculturation scales recommended with multicultural groups described in this book. If the therapist does not have enough time to conduct a thorough screening of acculturation using the scales in Chapter 8, Figure 2.1 provides a brief scale for the assessment of three significant variables in the process of acculturation: generation, language preferred, and social activity (Burnam, Hough, Karno, Escobar, & Telles, 1987; Cuellar, Harris, & Jasso, 1980; Suinn, Rickard-Figueroa, Lew, & Vigil, 1987). For example, family members in the fifth generation are considered highly acculturated in comparison with members in the first generation. In terms of language preferred, the client should be asked a general question regarding his or her preferred language in most situations (e.g., with children, with parents, and with coworkers). In the case of social activity, a similar approach is recommended. For example, a Mexican American client may be asked,

> When you listen to music and go to a restaurant to eat, would you do these things with Mexican Americans only, mostly with Mexican Americans, with Mexican Americans and other racial groups mostly (e.g., African Americans,

Instruction: Please check only one item from the group of generation items, language preferred items, and social activity items.

My generation is:

First	Second	Third	Fourth	Fifth
(1)	(2)	(3)	(4)	(5)

The language I prefer to use is:

Mine only	Mostly mine	Both mine and English	Mostly English	Only English
(1)	(2)	(3)	(4)	(5)

I prefer to engage in social activity:

Only within racial group	Mostly within racial group	Within/between racial groups	Mostly with a different racial group	Only with a different racial group
(1)	(2)	(3)	(4)	(5)

Total score: _____

Number of items checked: _____

Acculturation score (total score/number of items checked): _____

The level of acculturation for this client is (circle one):

Low	Medium	High

Figure 2.1. Brief Acculturation Scale

whites, Asians, and American Indians), with a different racial group of your own (e.g., whites), or only with a different racial group?

The following acculturation scores (suggested by Burnam et al., 1987) are recommended in the Brief Acculturation Scale:

1 to 1.75 = low acculturation

1.76 to 3.25 = medium acculturation

3.26 to 5 = high acculturation

To obtain these scores, add all values checked across variables and divide them by the total number of items checked. For example, if the client checked 1 for the first item across each variable, the total score would be 1 (3/3 = 1, or low acculturation score). If the client checked 2, 2, and 3 for the generational, language, and social activity variables, the overall acculturation score would be 2.3 (medium acculturation score).

Use of Translators

The use of translators is often necessary with clients with limited English proficiency. This is particularly true in the assessment and treatment of Asian American, Southeast Asian refugees, and Hispanic clients (Musser-Granski & Carrillo, 1997). Martinez (1986), however, recommends that clinicians should avoid the use of translators for two main reasons. First, the translator introduces a third person into the psychotherapy process, which could lead to distortion and misinterpretation of the client's verbalizations. Omissions, additions, and substitutions are examples of common distortions or errors associated with the process of translation in the practice of psychotherapy (Bamford, 1991; Musser-Granski & Carrillo, 1997). Second, clients may find the presence of the translator a disagreeable experience. Other findings include the inability of the translator to express the original speaker's thoughts, which could lead to confusing and misleading information; use of more severe psychiatric diagnoses when the client is not interviewed in his or her own language; increased drop-out rates from therapy because of the clients' inability to understand English; and increases in noncompliance behavior with therapist's recommendation (Seijo etal., 1991). Despite these negative findings, the use of translators may be an unavoidable issue in the practice of many clinicians. If translators are used, the following guidelines are recommended (Bamford, 1991; Gaw, 1993b; Ho, 1992; Westermeyer, 1993):

1. Clinicians should try to use translators who share the client's racial and ethnic background (e.g., Mexican American clients-Mexican American translators, and Cuban clients-Cuban translators), including an understanding of the variability in linguistic expressions within the same group (e.g., *mal puesto* among Mexican Americans and *brujeria* among Cubans).
2. Clinicians should use translators with training in mental health problems and culture-related syndromes (Chapter 9 provides examples of these syndromes).
3. Clinicians should use a sequential mode of translation (i.e., the client speaks, the translator translates into English, the therapist speaks, and the translator speaks again).
4. Clinicians should avoid concurrent translation (to prevent fatigue).

5. Clinicians should introduce the translator to the client and ensure that the translator spends time alone with the client talking about events common to both the translator and the client (e.g., their country of origin, and music) to provide the message that the translator can understand the client and facilitate the therapeutic alliance between the client and the therapist.

6. Clinicians should emphasize a sentence-by-sentence translation to avoid forgetting details.

7. Clinicians should avoid technical terms (e.g., "You probably have what we call dysthymia") and ask the client to describe in her or his own words the mental problem (e.g., "Tell me what exactly happened in the past two years when you say that you have been feeling very sad").

8. Clinical interview with translation will take twice as long. Thus, clinicians must plan ahead for the extra time needed for the translation. If the interview is terminated abruptly, the client may infer that the therapist is not interested in the case.

9. Clinicians should consider the potential effect of the translator during the interpretation of clinical data (i.e., the translator may function as a mediating variable affecting the relationship between reports of symptoms by the client and clinical diagnosis made by the clinician).

10. Clinicians should consider the level of acculturation of the translators in relation to the client's level of acculturation. The fact that a translator and a client share the same racial group (including sharing the same language) is extremely helpful in the evaluation process. Major discrepancies between the translator's level of acculturation and the client's level of acculturation, however, could create problems. For example, acculturated Hispanic translators who believe in the American way of dating may not appreciate the conflicts experienced by Hispanic parents who believe that it is not appropriate for their daughter to go out for a date alone or to engage in sexual relationships with a man without being married.

11. Clinicians should avoid the use of relatives and friends as translators. These translators are not often objective and could also distort the translation process to either minimize psychopathology or to maximize it depending on the context of therapy.

12. Clinicians should avoid the use of bilingual children as translators (particularly when the problem involves the child). Children's bilingualism could dramatically reverse the hierarchical role of parents who are monolingual or have a limited domain of English. This guideline is particularly important in the assessment and treatment of Hispanic and Asian families, in which the authority of parents (especially the father) cannot be reversed.

13. In the case of Asian clients, clinicians should determine the client's dialect before asking for a translator.

Overdiagnosing of Multicultural Groups

The possibility of overdiagnosing clients (i.e., false conclusions regarding "pathology" or mental problems) from any of the multicultural groups described in this book is an issue clinicians should always keep in mind (Chapter 9 includes further discussion on this issue). The error in "seeing" pathology or mental health problems in such groups has generally been explained in two ways. First, the psychometric properties of commonly used instruments for screening mental health problems are not generally appropriate for the assessment of similar problems among diversity groups (Dana, 1993b). Two important psychometric problems in the assessment of diversity groups discussed in this text are the use of inappropriate norms for the multicultural group and lack of cross-cultural validity (i.e., the instrument may not be sensitive in measuring the same mental problems with a group different from that used to originally develop the instrument).

The second explanation is associated with a lack of understanding regarding the impact of cultural variables, norms, and values on the development of behaviors resembling mental health problems (Dana, 1993b; Ramirez, Wassef, Paniagua, & Linskey, 1993). For example, it is not uncommon among Hispanic clients to report that they have "facultades espirituales" (spiritual faculties), meaning that they can communicate with "spirits" who live in an invisible world. A client with strong religious beliefs may claim that he or she can communicate with the saints through burning candles, praying, and so on. In addition, reports involving "having a conversation with the saints" or "receiving a verbal command from the Virgin Mary" are not uncommon among Hispanics. Spirit possession can also be reported by Asian and African American clients. For a clinician unfamiliar with these beliefs, such reports would be seen as examples of "severe psychopathology," when in fact these reports are only a function of the client's belief system (Bernal & Gutierrez, 1988; Dana, 1993b; Martinez, 1988).

Extended Family

Among African Americans, Hispanics, Asians, and American Indians, the phenomenon of the extended family seems to play a major role (Ho, 1992; McAdoo, 1993a; Pumariega et al., 1997; Sue & Sue, 1990). What is an extended family? The answer should be provided by the client and not by the therapist. An important guideline to remember is not to assume that the client and the therapist share the same definition of an extended family.

For example, it may be a mistake to assume that an aunt is viewed by an African American client as a member of the extended family (in the client's mind) simply because she is biologically related with the client. As noted by Anderson, Eaddy, and Williams (1990), the client would seek two types of supports before including an aunt in his or her definition of extended family: instrumental supports (e.g., money, clothing, or child care) and emotional supports (e.g., counseling and advice). If these supports cannot be provided by the aunt, she would not be included in the client's interpretation of an extended family.

A guideline for understanding the client's definition of "extension" in the interpretation of the client's extended family is to listen to the client's description of instrumental and emotional supports provided by any member of the community. Persons mentioned by the client with a fundamental role in the provision of such assistance should be considered in the client's extended family. These persons may include a brother (but not a sister), the priest (but not the grandfather), a friend (but not a uncle), or the case manager assigned to the client's case by welfare agencies (but not the director of these agencies).

The therapist should expect the client to bring to the clinic both biological (e.g., uncles, aunts, and sisters) and nonbiological (e.g., friends and the minister) members of his or her extended family. In the case of Hispanic clients, these nonbiological members often include the *compadre* (cofather) and the *comadre* (comother), who are invited by the client to play an active role in the process of psychotherapy (Comas-Díaz & Griffith, 1988). Among the American Indian clients, the elders in the tribe (particularly the head of the tribe) and traditional medicine men and women have a special place in the family, and they are also seen as an integral part of the extended family (Dana, 1993b; Ho, 1992; Richardson, 1981). In the case of African Americans, church membership is an essential element in the family, and it is expected that church members (particularly the minister) would be involved in the solution of family issues (Baker, 1988; Dana, 1993b). In this group, grandparents, sisters, and brothers often play a major role in the extended family (Boyd-Franklin, 1989). Among Asian American and Asian and Pacific Islander clients, the extended family does not generally include individuals (e.g., friends and minister) outside the core family structure (i.e., parents, children, grandparents, and relatives). This is because public admission of problems (including mental health problems) is generally not allowed in these groups (Sue & Sue, 1990). Finally, many Southeast Asian refugee clients (Vietnamese, Cambodians, and Laotians) may place more emphasize on the availability of nonbiological persons (e.g., friends) or social agencies (e.g., welfare agencies and community supports) in their definition of the extended family compared to an emphasis on the nuclear family (e.g., parents). The reason for this is that many refugees either left their family behind in their country of origin when they came to the United States, or their family members were killed during war (Mollica & Lavelle, 1988).

Implicit in the previous discussion is a distinction between the concepts of extended family tree and family tree. The latter term generally includes a description of the client and his or her immediate relatives (e.g., parents, siblings, and uncles). This approach is generally recommended in the formulation of the genogram (see Ho, 1987, p. 159). In clinical practice, however, the formulation of the family tree may not be a realistic approach in those cases in which the goal of the genogram is to describe the client's definition of the concept of extended family in terms of biological and nonbiological persons considered by the client as essential in the provision of instrumental and emotional supports. The formulation of the genogram in terms of the concept of extended family tree, however, may assist practitioners in approaching that definition because this concept includes both relatives and nonrelatives who provide such supports to the client during the time of crisis. For example, in the case of Hispanic clients, the extended family tree would include the client, children (if any), parents, grandparents, godfather, godmother, the priest, and friends. Similar extended family trees may be formulated for other multicultural groups with some variants. For example, in the case of American Indian clients, the medicine men and women would be included in that tree. In the case of Southeast Asian refugees, it is expected that more friends, social agencies, and case managers than relatives (e.g., parents) would be included in the extended family tree for reasons discussed previously.

Foster Homes and the Extended Family

Boyd-Franklin (1989) pointed out that no inquiry of the extended family could result in placing children in foster homes when the biological parents are not able to take care of them (e.g., because of hospitalization or severe father-mother marital conflicts that may put these children at risk for physical injuries). Therefore, it is important to ask parents about a member of the extended family (as it is defined by the client) who may be willing to take care of their child (or children) in those cases in which parents are not able to assume this responsibility. As noted earlier, the person selected by the client could be a nonbiological member of the extended family (e.g., a friend and the godfather). If foster parents (selected from the parents' extended family) and the biological parents do not share the same racial and ethnic background, the racial and ethnic identity of the child would be preserved in those cases in which the therapist ensures that foster parents understand the norms, values, beliefs, and other cultural aspects of the child's racial and ethnic background and apply that understanding in real-life situations. For example, in the case of African American children placed with white foster parents, special arrangements for the children to participate in activities involving other African American children (e.g., African American church activities) should be recommended (Jackson & Westmoreland, 1992). Similar arrangements are recommended with Hispanic, Asian, and American Indian children placed with foster parents from different racial and ethnic backgrounds. In the case of American Indian children, an additional guideline is strongly recommended: Do not handle foster care issues without an understanding of the Indian Child Welfare Act (discussed in Chapter 6).

Modality of Therapy

In general, African Americans, American Indians, Hispanics, and Asians prefer a therapy process that encompasses a directive approach (i.e., they want to know what is the problem and what to do to solve the problem), an active approach (i.e., what role would they play in the process of psychotherapy), and a structured approach (i.e., what exactly is the therapist recommending to solve the problem; Sue & Sue, 1990). Most forms of psychotherapies are recommended for multicultural groups described in this text, particularly behavioral approaches (e.g., social skills training) and family therapy (Ho, 1987; Tanaka-Matsumi & Higginbotham, 1996). Chapters 3 through 6 present examples of specific psychotherapies recommended for the four multicultural groups described in this book.

The programming of individual psychotherapy (i.e., interventions with only the client) is generally recommended with all groups prior to the scheduling of family therapy (a preferred form of intervention across groups in comparison with individual psychotherapy) in those cases in which the phenomenon of acculturation seems to play a major role in the manifestation of the clinical problem. This is particularly important to remember when the clinical problem involves either marital conflicts (e.g., discrepancies in values, norms, and worldview in less acculturated men compared to that of more acculturated women) or family problems involving children and adolescents with high levels of acculturation relative to their less acculturated parents. Jones (1992) pointed out that some African American adolescents are often referred for therapy because "their parents think they are mimicking maladaptive white adolescent behaviors (such as the wearing of punk-style haircuts or interest in heavy metal rock music" (p. 34). In this example, the assumption is that these African American adolescents may lose their racial and ethnic identity because of the impact of acculturation (i.e., the adoption of many of the behaviors of white adolescents). Jones recommended that individual psychotherapy sessions would be necessary "before initiating productive conjoint family therapy" (p. 34).

How Much Information Is Necessary?

Another general guideline is to avoid the collection of a very large amount of information. This guideline is particularly important during the first therapeutic contact with the client. The presenting problem, however, should always be emphasized but without giving the impression that too much information is needed to understand the problem. Most clients in such diverse groups (particularly Hispanics) view clinicians who collect a massive amount of information as incompetent both in technical (e.g., little training in collecting significant clinical data) and in cultural terms (unfamiliarity with the particular group; Seijo et al., 1991). The collection of an extensive amount of information is, of course, an essential strategy in the understanding of the client's problem. This level of information is particularly necessary when formulating the extended family tree. The important guideline to remember in this context, however, is to plan the collection of data gradually across sessions rather than giving the impression that you want to know everything in a 45-minute session. Factors that could facilitate extensive collection of clinical data after the first session with African American, Hispanic, Asian, and American Indian clients include the client's belief regarding the therapist's identification of the problem or problems that are considered by the client as essential, provision of concrete recommendations leading to the solution of such problems through an emphasis on problem-solving techniques, and the client's perception of credibility. In the absence of such factors, it would be difficult to gather extensive clinical data beyond the preliminary clinical data collected during the first session (e.g., an overview of the problem and perhaps some information about other family members).

The Meaning of "Therapist"
Across Multicultural Groups

Familiarity with the use of the term *therapist* across multicultural groups is recommended. For example, many Asians and African Americans view their therapist as a "physician"; for the American Indians, the therapist is a medicine man or a medicine woman; and many Hispanics would treat the therapist as a "folk healer" (Comas-Díaz & Griffith, 1988; Ho, 1992; Sue & Sue, 1990).

Understanding the client's definition of therapist could greatly enhance the clinician's ability to manage the problem For example, American Indian clients do not expect the therapist to recommend synthetic medication for their mental problems; natural herbs are expected. By contrast, many Asian and African American clients would expect a discussion of how synthetic medication could control their problems. In the first case, the therapist may be viewed as the medicine man, whereas in the second case, the client may perceive the role of the therapist as a physician (Baker, 1988; Richardson, 1981; Sue & Sue, 1990).

3

Guidelines for the Assessment and Treatment of African American Clients

In 1995, the African American population was approximately 33.6 million (U.S. Bureau of the Census, 1996). The majority of African Americans live in the South, and smaller numbers live in the north central, northeast, and western regions of the United States (U.S. Department of Health & Human Services, 1991). The median income of African American families in 1995 was $24,698, which was below the national U.S. average of $39,276 and below that of whites ($40,884; U.S. Bureau of the Census, 1996). In 1995, the incomes of 27.3% of African American families and 30.6% of African American persons were below the poverty line (U.S. Bureau of the Census, 1996) in comparison with the incomes of 9.1% of white families and 11.7% of white persons below the poverty level.

Guidelines on Cultural Variables That May Affect Assessment and Treatment of African American Clients

Racial Labels

Racial labels have been a concern to African Americans for many years (Smith, 1992). Members of this group have been called Colored, Negro,

20

black, and African American (Smith, 1992). The first three terms emphasize skin color. The last term emphasizes cultural heritage, and it is currently recommended in the literature (Griffith & Baker, 1993; Smith, 1992). The terms Colored and Negro are considered derogatory and should not be used by practitioners (Smith, 1992). The terms black and African American seem acceptable within a given context. For example, Karkabi (1993) published an interview in the *Houston Chronicle* dealing with the use of both terms; one of the interviewees reported,

> If a brother or sister wants to call me black, that's OK. But I would prefer that Anglo call me African American. . . . It acknowledges our ancestry and where we came from, and I think that use of that term by Anglo is more respectful. (p. 5D)

It seems appropriate for a therapist to explore which term (black or African American) is preferred by a client. A practical strategy is to ask the client directly about his or her choice. Some clients prefer to be called black, and others prefer the term African American. In both cases, the therapist should honor the wish of the client and stay neutral with respect to current controversies regarding the use of such terms (Smith, 1992, provides an excellent summary of this controversy).

The term African American is used in this book because it is gaining acceptability in the literature (Dana, 1993b; Griffith & Baker, 1993; Ho, 1992; Smith, 1992). Several reasons have been suggested for selecting the term African American: It is less stigmatizing (Dana, 1993b), it does not emphasize skin color but includes reference to cultural heritage (Griffith & Baker, 1993), and it formalizes the African connection (Fairchild, 1985).

Familism and Role Flexibility

Both the nuclear family (parents and children) and the extended family (parents, children, relatives, friends, the minister, etc.) are important among African Americans (Boyd-Franklin, 1989; Smith, 1981). Because the concept of familism among African Americans generally includes both biological (e.g., parents, children, uncles, and sisters) and nonbiological (e.g., friends, minister, and godfather) members, an important guideline to follow with this group is to formulate a genogram emphasizing the extended family tree (as defined in Chapter 2) rather than simply the biological family tree (a similar guideline is recommended for American Indian, Asian, and Hispanic clients).

Who is the head of the family? Among African American clients, the head of the family is not necessarily the father (Baker, 1988). An important issue in these families is role flexibility: The mother sometimes plays the role of the father and thus functions as the head of the family. In addition, older children sometimes function as parents or caretakers for younger children. In fact, older African American children may drop out from school to work and help younger children secure a good education (Baker, 1988; Ho, 1992; Smith, 1981). This practice should be carefully considered when a therapist is conducting family therapy with family members involving adolescents; the therapist should not assume that an African American adolescent dropped out of school because of the problem that parents bring to the attention of the therapist.

As noted by Boyd-Franklin (1989), the concept of role flexibility among African American families can be extended to include the parental role assumed by grandfather, grandmother, aunts, and cousins. Therefore, an assessment of an African American client should include the identification of the head of the family at the moment of the referral.

Religious Beliefs

For many African American families, the church (particularly an African American church) is considered an important member of the extended family (Griffith, English, & Mayfield, 1980; Levin & Taylor, 1993). Therefore, an important guideline is to explore the role that the church plays in the life of an African American client. An initial approach is to determine the client's particular church affiliation. Examples of church affiliation generally reported by African American clients include Baptist, African Methodist Episcopal, Jehovah's Witness, Church of God in Christ, Seventh Day Adventist, Pentecostal, Apostolic, Presbyterian, Lutheran, Episcopal, Roman Catholic, and Nation of Islam. The majority of African American clients belong to the Baptist and the African Methodist Episcopal churches (Boyd-Franklin, 1989).

Despite the central role that the church plays in the lives of many African Americans (Smith, 1981), it is important to avoid the generalization of this point for all African American clients seen in therapy. A second approach is to explore whether the particular client includes the church in his or her extended family. One way to investigate this is to ask, "Have you discussed your emotional problems with someone in your church?" "Someone" could be anybody (e.g., a friend, a minister, or a priest). If church members are essential in providing instrumental and emotional supports (according to the client), the therapist could ask, "Would you like to include these church members in our discussion of your concerns?"

Folk Beliefs

Some African American clients believe that folk medicine can be effective in the treatment of their medical and mental problems (Baker & Lightfoot, 1993; Wilkinson & Spurlock, 1986). Within the belief systems of many African Americans, mental problems can not only be the result of physical causes but also be determined by occult or spiritual factors. If the illness has a physical cause, it could be cured with herbs, teas, and other natural substances, and folk doctors are often consulted for treatment. If the illness is the result of occult or spiritual factors (including evil spirits, supernatural forces, violation of sacred beliefs, or sin), folk healers are consulted for treatment (Dana, 1993b).

When African American clients seek help for their mental health problems, four types of healers are often available. The old lady generally deals with common ailments, provides advice, gives medication (e.g., the use of herbs), and is most often consulted by young mothers. The spiritualist is the most common folk healer among African Americans seeking help with their problems. The voodoo priest or *hougan* has more formal training in the process of healing (including selection of plants for healing purposes and prescribing the ingestion of organs or parts of certain animals to treat the problem) and has the skills to deal with individual and family problems. In addition, many African American clients believe that the solution to these problems should include the client's involvement with Bible study groups, prayer meetings, and advice from the minister (Dana, 1993b). To enhance the assessment and treatment of African American clients, it would be a good tactic to accept these beliefs regarding the client's understanding of causation of mental health problems and their solution (Baker & Lightfoot, 1993; Smith, 1981).

Healthy Paranoia

Slavery and racism are two important factors in the history of African Americans in the United States that have dramatically shaped the social and psychological development of this group over time (Gregory, 1996; Smith, 1981). An important consequence of this is the development of the healthy cultural paranoia phenomenon (Ho, 1992; Smith, 1981). African Americans present themselves as highly suspicious of others with different color and values; this could interfere with the client-therapist relationship. If the therapist perceives that the client does not trust him or her and requests an explanation for the healthy cultural paranoia instead of demonstrating an understanding of this phenomenon in historical terms, the client may perceive the therapist as culturally insensitive.

The Language of African American Clients

Communicative exchange between the client and therapist is an essential element in the process of psychotherapy. This point applies to all forms of therapy and not only to those therapies termed "talk therapy." Communicative exchange could be difficult to fulfill in those cases in which the client uses words, sentences, a syntax, and phonology that are not part of the language of the therapist (Wilkinson & Spurlock, 1986). This point is particularly important to remember in the assessment and treatment of African American clients who may use Black English (instead of Standard American English) or street talk during the therapeutic process. Practitioners are encouraged to consult Dillard (1973) and Smitherman (1995), who provide a wide variety of examples demonstrating that distinction.

For example, in terms of grammar, the question "Have they gone there?" (Standard American English) would be replaced by "Is they gone there?" using Black English (Dillard, 1973, p. 49). In other cases, what is at issue is the meaning of the particular sentence. For example, if an African American mother reports "My child sick" and another African American mother reports "My child be sick," the meaning of the first sentence is that the child is currently sick and the sickness is of short-term duration; the second sentence, however, indicates that the child has been sick for a long time (Dillard, 1973). The reason for this is that in Black English, the term "be" is used to "indicate continuous action or infrequently occurring activity" (Smitherman, 1995, p. 7), which is the case in the second example.

The use of street talk is another point to consider in the assessment and treatment of African American clients. In this case, the speaker (e.g., the client) may or may not use Standard American English, but the listener (e.g., the therapist) may have problems understanding words or sentences used by the speaker. For example, the sentence, "I would like to have plenty of bank to buy a hog to go to Cali," is grammatically correct in Standard American English, but the listener will not understand this sentence unless he or she is familiar with the slang words bank (money), hog (Cadillac or, more generally, a car), and Cali (California; Dillard, 1973, p. 240; Smitherman, 1995, pp. 54, 75, 135). Additional examples of slang in street-talk black include the following: "I was mad of her because she was not clean," in which "clean" in this specific case means dressed up or stylishly dressed; "If I get a gig, I will feel better" (gig means job); and "He likes to rap with the dude who lives across the street" (rap means talk, and dude means man).

The following is the basic guideline: If you cannot understand the language of an African American client, you should ask the client directly about what you exactly do not understand (e.g., a word or the meaning of a sentence). Several African Americans who consulted for this portion of this book reported that, in many instances, they also a have problem understanding Black English and street talk. Thus, therapists who cannot understand the language of an African American client should not feel embarrassed to ask questions to enhance communication between themselves and clients who use Black English or street talk. A variant of this guideline is that the African American client must understand that the therapist is not questioning the correctness of Black English (in comparison with Standard American English) or the particular word. The client must understand, both verbally and nonverbally, that the main goal of such questions or inquiries is to facilitate verbal exchanges (communication) between the therapist and the client, which is a crucial element in understanding the client's main concerns.

The First Session

The first session with any client sets the tone for a healthy client-therapist relationship in subsequent sessions (Baker, 1988; Ho, 1992; Smith, 1981). The literature suggests specific guidelines dealing with the use of cultural skills during the first encounter between an African American client and a therapist.

Discussion of Racial Differences

Because of the African American history of racism and discrimination by the dominant Anglo-American culture, an African American client referred to an Anglo-American therapist would come to the first session with the belief that the therapist is an "alien" and that he or she will not be able to understand the problem because of racial differences. To minimize these feelings, during the first session, the therapist should first acknowledge that difference and encourage the client to talk about his or her feelings concerning this issue. Racial issues, however, should not be discussed during brief or emergency interventions involving a crisis (Wilkinson & Spurlock, 1986).

In those cases in which the therapist is white and the client is an African American, a suggested approach to begin talking about racial differences during the first session is to say, "Some African American clients feel uncomfortable when they are referred to a white therapist. Perhaps we could briefly talk about feelings you may have regarding our racial differences." Another statement suggested by Boyd-Franklin (1989) is, "How do you feel about working with a white therapist?" (p. 102). These general comments may not only reduce racial tension between the client and the therapist but also help the therapist to appear less anxious, more comfortable, and sensitive to the client's expectations and beliefs (Baker, 1988). In addition, when racial differences are openly discussed with African American clients, the therapist may give the impression that the client can discuss anything in that session in a safe environment.

Another important guideline is to avoid discussion of racial issues in subsequent sessions (unless the client brings them to the attention of the therapist). If a repetition of similar issues continues after the first session, the therapist may convey to the African American client the impression that he or she is anxious about the potential effects of cross-racial issues and that this anxiety may interfere with the ability of the therapist to effectively assess and treat the client (Boyd-Franklin, 1989).

Why Should an African American Therapist Discuss Racial Issues With an African American Client?

In cases in which the client and the therapist are African Americans, the assumption is that because of this shared racial status the client would be less suspicious and guarded, more relaxed, and more open to discuss personal problems with the therapist. In this circumstance, it appears unnecessary to recommend a discussion of racial issues with an African American client. This conclusion, however, may not be totally true (Boyd-Franklin, 1989; Wilkinson & Spurlock, 1986). For example, Boyd-Franklin (1989) points out that because of the "macho" belief among many African Americans, a client from this group would find it difficult to openly discuss personal matters in front of an African American therapist. In addition, an African American client treated by a therapist from the same race could also "check out" the therapist (i.e., attention to nonverbal cues suggesting that the therapist is distancing himself or herself from the client) and display the same "healthy cultural paranoid" phenomenon generally assumed in those cases in which African American clients are seen by white therapists.

One important guideline for an African American therapist treating a client from the same race is to avoid thinking that racial similarity will necessarily enhance (or guarantee) the therapist-client therapeutic relationship. In this specific case, the therapist should present a set of verbal and nonverbal behaviors leading to the establishment of himself or herself as a peer rather than assuming that the client will consider the therapist as a peer simply because he or she is an African American therapist. A useful statement to indicate that the African American therapist is interested in discussing racial issues with a client from the same race would be the following: "African

Americans sometimes feel uncomfortable discussing mental problems with African American mental health professionals. Because I am an African American [or black, depending on the client's preference of the terms], I wonder if you feel the same way with me?" To facilitate a verbal exchange between the client and the therapist regarding this particular issue, it is recommended that the therapist avoid sitting behind a desk to signal to an African American client that the therapist does not want to distance himself or herself from the client and to convey the sense that discussion of racial issues will be taken very seriously by the therapist. This physical arrangement is recommended throughout the entire process of therapy to continue the development of trust between the client and the therapist (Boyd-Franklin, 1989).

It is important to make a distinction between a discussion of racial issues to facilitate assessment and treatment during the first session and the therapist's (explicit or implicit) role as a "protector of the race" (Boyd-Franklin 1989). African American clients are aware of their history of rejection, racism, and slavery in the United States. Thus, an African American client may become suspicious of African American therapists who, in the process of assessment and treatment, present themselves as members of this race with the education and training to "preach and teach" African American clients. Therefore, in addition to scheduling a brief period to discuss racial issues, it is also important to avoid mixing discussion of racial issues leading to the development of the therapist-client therapeutic relationship with discussions involving political or racial problems in society.

Regardless of the race of the therapist, a discussion of racial differences during the first therapy session does not necessarily guarantee the enhancement of the therapist-client relationship in subsequent sessions. As noted by Wilkinson and Spurlock (1986), "the therapist's openness, sensitivity, and ability . . . training and experience, are generally more important" (p. 51).

Explore the Level of Acculturation

The fact that a client is an African American does not mean that the client himself or herself feels that way (Dana, 1993b; Ho, 1992). Some African American clients prefer to identify with the Anglo-American culture and may display many behavior patterns like those displayed by the Anglo-American community (e.g., dress, music, and language). This preference may be acquired through the process of internal acculturation described previously, which should be explored to determine an African American client's perception of identity with the dominant culture versus the client's perception of racial identity with his or her own race (Sue & Sue, 1990). One way to explore this point is by encouraging the client to talk about his or her past and current experiences with the African American community versus his or her experiences with the Anglo-American community. In addition, the Brief Acculturation Scale described in Chapter 2 (Figure 2.1) may be useful.

Avoid Causal Explanations of Problems

In general, African American clients believe that emotional problems are caused by environmental factors. Thus, linking the mental health problem with parents' behavior (or with other members of the extended family), for example, is not a good tactic when working with African American clients. The best approach would be to avoid explanation regarding the origin of the problem during the first session. During this session, African American clients generally prefer concrete suggestion regarding the solution to their mental problems rather than long and complex explanation regarding the origin of these problems (Baker, 1988).

Include the Church in the
Assessment and Therapy Processes

The church plays a major role in the life of African Americans (Griffith et al., 1980; Taylor & Chatters, 1986). This observation is particularly important to remember in the assessment and treatment of African American women because they tend to show more involvement with church activities in comparison with African American men (Levin & Taylor, 1993). Thus, a practical guideline is to assess whether the client is a member of a particular church and the availability of economic and emotional supports from the particular church. The next step is to inform the client that he or she may bring church members to subsequent meetings to help with the assessment and treatment of the client's concerns (e.g., "If you believe that someone in your church should be invited to discuss this problem with both you and me, please let me know about this possibility and I will be glad to extend an invitation to that person"). If, prior to the first meeting, the therapist is aware (e.g., through information given by the client on the phone when scheduling the first meeting) that the client belongs to one of the churches in the community, the client should be told either on the phone or in writing that it will be acceptable if he or she would like to bring any church member during the first meeting. It is also important to inform the staff (e.g., secretaries and mental health paraprofessionals) about this guideline because in many instances, the therapist is not the person making the first contact with the African American when he or she calls the clinic to make an appointment.

With African American clients who are new residents in the community, it is important to explore whether the client has already found a church that could fulfill his or her religious needs. Of course, one should be familiar with the churches (as listed previously) available in that particular community. A good approach is to have a listing with the name, phone number, and address of each church that can be made available to new African American residents in the community. As noted by Boyd-Franklin (1989), helping an African American client to find a church may play a significant role in the process of psychotherapy (e.g., the minister may help in encouraging an African American client to come back for therapy or to follow the therapist's recommendations). In addition, this type of assistance may greatly enhance the therapist-client therapeutic relationship.

Define the Role of Those Accompanying the Client

Many African Americans bring members of the extended family (biological or nonbiological members) to the initial interview because they expect that the therapist will allow the presence of such members during that interview (Baker, 1988). These invited (by the client) members often include relatives (uncles and aunts) and nonrelatives (friends, godfather, church members, etc.). To avoid making false assumptions about the role of these people during the first session, it is important to clarify that role prior to the assessment of the case. The main concern here is to determine situations in which these extended family members could help in the evaluation and treatment of an African American client (Griffith & Baker, 1993). This guideline is particularly important to remember in those cases in which the grandmother comes to the first meeting. The grandmother is probably the second most important member in the extended family (Boyd-Franklin, 1989). Thus, the presence of the grandmother in that meeting is often a sign of social or spiritual support or both.

In many African American families, the primary caretaker is not the mother but the grandmother. If the grandmother brings the child for assessment and treatment to the clinic, however, she may show lack of understanding of fundamental psychological and developmental processes relevant in the assessment and treatment of the child. Despite this lack of understanding, the grandmother would make major decisions regarding the child's life. Thus, the therapist should expect that recommendations for assessment and treatment may not be followed by the mother without the approval of her own mother. For this reason, in the assessment and treatment of African American children, an important guideline to consider is to quickly explore the role of the grandmother in the child's life in that session. If the therapist perceives that this role is crucial, the grandmother should be invited to attend subsequent therapy sessions and invited to actively participate in the assessment and treatment of the case.

Use a Present-Time Focus Approach

During the first session, an African American client will discuss both the core or most essential problem he or she feels should be considered first and additional problems that may be handled in later sessions (Baker, 1988). For the "core" problem, the client would expect the therapist to suggest a focused, brief intervention to deal with that problem quickly.

Screen Carefully for Depression

Griffith and Baker (1993) suggested that the myth that African Americans cannot become depressed could result in the underdiagnosis of depression in this group. These authors recommend the screening of the following criteria before concluding that an African American client does not have major depression:

1. Neurovegative signs (e.g., weight loss and fatigue)
2. Client's view of the future
3. Past and current sources of pleasures from specific persons
4. Level of productivity
5. Degree of participation in church activities
6. Degree of participation as caregivers for younger family members

Avoid Misdiagnosing Substance Abuse Syndromes as Schizophrenia

Griffith and Baker (1993) noted that the high prevalence of schizophrenia reported among African American clients may be the result of a history of substance abuse. Hallucinations and delusions are the key symptoms in a diagnosis of schizophrenia. These symptoms, however, can also result from chronic alcoholism and the use of illicit drugs (e.g., cocaine, heroin, cocaine derivative, or crack). Thus, during the first session with an African American client, it is recommended to screen for a history of substance abuse. If this client comes to the clinic with symptoms of schizophrenia and these symptoms disappear within approximately 2 hours in the absence of treatment (e.g., medication), the client probably has experienced a cocaine psychosis.

In this case, failure to screen for substance abuse would lead to an error in diagnosing that client with schizophrenia.

Handle Family Secrets With Care

During the first session with an African American client, it is important to be sensitive to the possibility of family secrets. The key point in dealing with family secrets among African Americans is to wait for the natural revelation of these secrets over time because, in most cases, that revelation is simply a matter of timing (Boyd-Franklin, 1989). Family secrets can take many forms, including reasons for adoption (i.e., why the child was adopted by his aunt), use of drugs by parents (and other members of the family), past problems with the police leading to arrest and conviction, and secrets regarding fatherhood (Boyd-Franklin, 1989).

There are specific guidelines in the literature regarding methods to identify these secrets during the first session as well as general guidelines concerning appropriate ways to handle these secrets. For example, if the grandmother brings a child to the clinic and she states that she has adopted the child without providing a reason for the adoption, one may suspect a family secret. Also, if an adolescent asks his parents in the presence of the therapist, "Why do I look different from my brothers?" and the therapist senses that the parents avoid the question, this could also be a case of family secrets. If the therapist says, "Mr. Brown, could you tell me about your life when you were an adolescent?" and he replies, "I don't feel like talking about this now," another family secret might be suspected.

The basic guideline in the identification of suspected family secrets includes three elements: listen carefully to what the client says, attend to the amount of silence when the client is questioned about an issue that appears to be sensitive, and do not ask questions that may imply the revelation of family secrets. For example, during the first session, practitioners generally expect parents to be present to register a child and sign documents dealing with consent for assessment and treatment. If a parent (either the mother or the father) is not present to fulfill this task, it would be inappropriate to ask a grandparent, an adult brother or sister, or an adult aunt or uncle, "Why is Sue's mother not here today?" This question may seem appropriate to the therapist but could be an invitation to discuss a secret prematurely, and the result could be attrition (i.e., the family may not come back for additional sessions).

In this circumstance, three steps are recommended. First, inquire about the relationship between the child and the person(s) seeking help for the child (e.g., a grandparent) to determine the person's legal guardian status with the case. Second, clearly state that if that person is not the legal guardian, the child will be seen to determine if there is an emergency that requires immediate attention (e.g., suicide attempts). If that person states that he or she is not the legal guardian, the following comment is suggested:

> I am very pleased that you brought Sue to this clinic today, which shows that you care about her. I will see Sue to determine that she is not a danger to herself or to others. In the next session, it would be helpful if you could bring Sue's legal guardian to sign consent for further assessment and therapy.

This statement not only avoids questions dealing with family secrets but also provides that person with the opportunity to mention the child's legal guardian without pressure from the therapist. The third step is for the therapist to be familiar with state laws and regulations regarding consent in the assessment and treatment of children and adolescents. For example, in Texas, a family member (e.g., a grandparent or an adult brother or sister) may consent for the treatment of a child "when the person having the power to consent . . . cannot be contacted and actual notice to the contrary has not been given by that person" (Costello & Hays, 1988, p. 87).

Do Not Try Hard to
Understand African American Clients

In a workshop dealing with the assessment and treatment of African American clients (scheduled by the Texas Psychological Association), presenters made the following recommendation: "If you try hard to understand African Americans, then you do not understand them at all." The same suggestion can be found in Boyd-Franklin (1989). For example, an Anglo therapist may use slangs that he or she believes are representative of African American dialect. In this example, the intention of the therapist is to make a "attempt to join with the [African American] family" (Boyd-Franklin, 1989, p. 100). This approach, however, is not recommended with African American clients for two reasons. First, the therapist may use a slang in an inappropriate context. Second, this approach may be considered by African American clients as condescending.

Do Not Emphasize Deficits;
Emphasize Strengths

During the first session with an African American client, it is important to avoid any suggestion (either verbally or nonverbally) leading to the assumption that the client comes from a disorganized, unstable, or psychologically unhealthy family because of the client's color. This characterization of African American families was the prevalent view during the 1960s, and it has been challenged during the past 20 years. For example, the assumption that a stable, organized, and psychologically healthy family "must consist of two parents" (Boyd-Franklin, 1989, p. 15) suggests that any family lacking this attribute is inherently pathological. Because these attributes are not shared by many African American families (many of which are headed by single mothers), the conclusion would be that these families are disorganized, unstable, and psychologically unhealthy. This conclusion is not only untrue (Wilkinson & Spurlock, 1986) but also does not take into consideration the role of other factors (e.g., the role of the extended family, role flexibility in many African American families, strong religious orientation, and strong emphasis on the value of education) that can lead to family functioning in those cases in which the African American family is headed by a single parent. These factors are the strengths of African American family that the therapist should emphasize and use in subsequent therapy sessions to encourage African American families to participate in therapy (Boyd-Franklin, 1989).

In the case of the role of the extended family, many African American mothers report during the first session that they are single mothers. If the therapist does not further explore the definition of "extended family" in the mind of the client, the role of a potential stepfather may not be revealed by the mother. In this example, the stepfather may play an essential role in the development and maintenance of family functioning during the process of psychotherapy. This role, however, would not be revealed until the therapist explores the impact of the extended family (as the concept was defined in Chapter 2).

Conducting Psychotherapy

The previous guidelines are recommended during the first therapeutic contact with African American clients in which the emphasis is placed on the collection of preliminary clinical data with minimal emphasis on the psychotherapy process. If the client returns for psychotherapy in subsequent sessions (Chapter 7 summarizes guidelines to prevent attrition or dropping out from therapy), another set of guidelines is recommended in the literature (Baker, 1988; Boyd-Franklin, 1989; Dana, 1993b; Griffith & Baker, 1993; Ho, 1992; Lefley & Pedersen, 1986; Smith, 1981).

Emphasize Empowerment

During the course of therapy with an African American client, it is important to reinforce the concept of "empowerment" and to relate this concept with the client's experience of therapeutic changes. This concept is important with any family regardless of cultural background. In the case of the African American clients, however, the concept plays an important role because of a long history of slavery, racism, and discrimination experienced by this group in the United States. Two major goals a therapist would want to accomplish when dealing with this concept in psychotherapy are (a) to help the client to gain the skills necessary to make important decisions in his or her own life and the lives of the other family members (including children, spouse, and extended family members), and (b) to assist the client in the development of skills that could help the client to take back control of his or her family.

For example, an African American client may experience a sense of powerlessness because, in his or her mind, he or she does not have the right to select a therapist in those cases in which the client is referred for therapy by a welfare agency. In this example, the therapist's task is to be sensitive to that sense of powerlessness (e.g., "I understand that you feel that you cannot make a decision regarding the selection of a therapist of your choice") and to make clear that specific techniques to develop skills to deal with these feelings will be discussed during the process of psychotherapy (e.g., the use of problem-solving and social skills training to reestablish power).

Recommended Modalities of Therapy

Problem-Solving and Social Skills Training

The central goal of problem-solving training is to teach people to quickly deal with the solution of one or more problems in a series of problems (Kratochwill & Bergan, 1990). Because the therapist teaches the client how to resolve his or her own problems using problem-solving techniques, this strategy may be perceived by the client as a way of taking back power (or control) over his or her own behavior or over other family members. In general, African American clients (and other multicultural groups) generally expect a quick solution to problems they identify as essential (among a set of target problems). Therefore, as these problems are identified and solved with problem-solving techniques, the development of credibility (e.g., the feeling that the therapist knows what to do with this particular client and his or her problems) and a sense of trust toward the therapist is facilitated over time (Boyd-Franklin, 1989).

Teaching clients to be assertive by using appropriate social skills is the main goal of social skills training (Lange & Jakubowski, 1976). As noted by Yamamoto, Silva, Chang, and Leong (1993), many members of culturally diverse groups "feel they cannot speak up or assert themselves. Despite improving race relations, [diverse groups] often express that they still feel as if they are *second-class citizens* [italics added]" (p. 116). Social skills training is recommended with African American clients who are not assertive in their interpersonal relationships with other people (including family members) because of fear of negative consequences (rejection, verbal reprimands, etc.) or believe that they do not have the right to express their reactions to other people with "power" outside the extended family.

Family Therapy

As noted previously, the extended family plays a major role in the lives of many African American clients. For this reason, several authors suggest that family therapy should be considered among the first treatment approaches with African American clients (Boyd-Franklin, 1989, pp. 141-142). All forms of family therapy are recommended with African American families. There are, however, two tactics recommended with any form of family therapy scheduled with African American families (Boyd-Franklin, 1989, pp. 141-142). The first tactic is an emphasis on the assignment of tasks that the family should conduct at home and then report to the therapist in subsequent sessions. This tactic not only allows the therapist to deal with the solution of the problem in the target setting (e.g., at home) but also may encourage other family members (who refuse to come to family therapy) to participate (or to be more active) in the process of family therapy. In addition, because many African American clients enter treatment looking for a "quick fix" to their problems (Boyd-Franklin, 1989), the assignment of tasks could be seen by these clients as an example of the therapist's interest in "quickly dealing with the problem."

The second tactic is the scheduling of role-play scenarios to develop communication among family members. Many African American clients are not familiar with the concept of "family therapy" as something that can actually help them in solving their problems. Several family therapy sessions are recommended to encourage each family member to role play the way he or she might talk about the target problem at home and how all members could find solutions to that particular problem only when they elect to communicate their feelings and concerns to other family members. One important consequence of role playing in family therapy with this group is that this tactic could enhance the therapist's ability to reestablish the sense of power or control in the family. That is, by learning how to communicate and solve problems in role-playing scenarios, an African American client would also learn that the "powerlessness" and "weakness" he or she experienced prior to family therapy could gradually be transformed into a sense of empowerment or control. Boyd-Franklin (1989) suggests that the reestablishment of this sense of control should be seen as a fundamental task in any form of family therapy in the treatment of African American clients.

When the goal of family therapy is to deal with emotional problems among African American couples (e.g., husband and wife), additional guidelines are recommended. In general, when white couples seek help from a therapist, both partners mutually agree to discuss their problems with a therapist. As noted by Boyd-Franklin (1989), this level of agreement "is exceedingly rare among [African American] people" (p. 225). Boyd-Franklin suggests that this observation could be explained in terms of the socialization of African American men, in which the impact of racism, discrimination, and the development of the macho role prevent men from showing weakness during difficult times. These factors could have major implications in couple relationships between African American men and women. The admission of emotional problems and reports about these problems to people outside the family network (e.g., the therapist) may be interpreted as a sign of weakness in the minds of many African American men.

Thus, assuming that the man came to the first family therapy session, a major problem that the therapist may have to confront during subsequent sessions with an African American couple is to determine strategies to encourage the man to return for therapy. Boyd-Franklin (1989) has provided a series of general guidelines for engaging African American men in family therapy. First, the therapist should signal to the woman that she could be seen alone. Second, it is important to explore the woman's understanding of her partner's position with respect to therapy for their mutual problems.

Third, although giving the man an ultimatum by her partner (e.g., "If you do not come to therapy, I will leave you") may be a good approach to bring the man to therapy, it is important to inform the woman that this approach may signal to the man that he is being "forced" to come to therapy and that as a result of this "forced-choice" tactic, the man may feel that he may lose his autonomy and the power to choose his own ways of confronting and resolving the problem. Fourth, it is important for the woman to understand that it may help if the therapist talks to the man directly. A time and day when the man could be reached on the phone should be determined in that session, and the woman should be instructed to inform her partner that the therapist will call him at that particular time and day. The therapist should emphasize that he or she wants to talk to the man directly instead of using the woman as the "messenger." Because of the general negative attitude toward therapy and the cultural paranoid phenomenon among African Americans, during the first phone conversation with the man, it is important that the therapist tell the man that he or she has discussed the problem with the man's partner (e.g., the wife) and that the main purpose of this conversation is to explore his ideas, suggestions, or understanding with respect to the target problem (i.e., only the problem mentioned by the woman to the therapist). The therapist should also emphasize that this information is needed to assist (avoid the term help) the couple in the solution of their concerns (avoid the term problem).

4

Guidelines for the Assessment and Treatment of Hispanic Clients

The second largest multicultural group in mental health services includes the Hispanics. In 1995, the total number of Hispanics was approximately 28.3 million (U.S. Bureau of the Census, 1996). The majority of Hispanics were Mexican Americans (approximately 18.0 million), Puerto Ricans (2.8 million), and Cubans (1.2 million). It is estimated that by the year 2020, between 47 million and 54.3 million Hispanics will be residing in the United States (Dana, 1993b; Marin & Marin, 1991). The majority of Hispanics (approximately 86%) in the United States live in urban areas (Marin & Marin, 1991).

In summarizing the data from the 1982 U.S. Census, Marin and Marin (1991) noted that the majority of four subgroups of Hispanics (Mexican Americans, Cubans, Puerto Ricans, and Dominicans) resided in four states: California (31.1%), Texas (20.4%), New York (11.4%), and Florida (5.9%). Most Mexican Americans live in southwestern states (Arizona, California, Colorado, New Mexico, and Texas). The majority of Cubans live in Florida (mainly in Miami); the majority of Puerto Ricans and Dominicans live in the New York and New Jersey areas. Other Hispanics from Central American (e.g., Panama, Costa Rica, and Nicaragua) and South American (e.g., Colombia and Venezuela) countries are residing mostly in New York City and San Francisco (Marin & Marin, 1991).

In 1995, the median income for Hispanic families (including Mexican Americans, Cubans, Puerto Ricans, Central and South American Hispanics, and other Hispanics) was $24,313, below the national median of $39,276 and in comparison to $40,884 for white families (U.S. Bureau of the Census, 1996). It should be noted that in 1995, the median income for Hispanics was lower than the median income for African Americans (i.e., $24,698). Among the larger subgroups of Hispanics in the United States, the Cubans reported the highest median income level in 1995 ($30,584) and the Puerto Ricans reported the lowest level ($20,929). In 1995, the incomes of approximately 27.8% of Hispanic families and 30.7% of Hispanic persons were below the poverty level in comparison with those of 9.1% of white families and 11.7% of white persons. The Cubans reported the lowest percentage of families below the poverty level in 1995—13.6% (U.S. Bureau of the Census, 1996).

Terminology

In general, a person is considered "Hispanic" in terms of language skill (Spanish speaking), family name (Spanish surname), or ancestry (Spanish American). Ruiz and Padilla (1977) used the concept of Hispanics to include all persons of "Spanish origin and descent." A more inclusive definition of Hispanics was provided by Marin and Marin (1991): "Individuals who reside in the United States and who were born in or trace the background of their families to one of the Spanish-speaking Latin American nations or Spain" (p. 1). These persons would include people from Spain, Central American countries (e.g., Mexico, Panama, and Costa Rica), South American countries (e.g., Venezuela and Colombia), and the Caribbean (e.g., Puerto Rico and Cuba).

Two additional terms commonly used in the current context are Latino and Hispanic American. The first term implies that a person is from a Latin American country (e.g., from Cuba) and, as noted by Dana (1993b), Mexican Americans tend to prefer this term because it "does not signify the conqueror Spain" (p. 66). The second term implies that a person is not only of Spanish origin but also that he or she was born in the United States. Currently, the literature suggests that most investigators prefer the term Hispanics in its most overall sense (Dana, 1993b; Ho, 1992; Marin & Marin, 1991; Ruiz, 1981), including people who label themselves as Hispanics because they are from Spain, from any of the South American or Central American nations, or from the Caribbean. Because many people who consider themselves Hispanics do not speak Spanish, it may not be appropriate to label a person Hispanic on the basis of the ability to speak Spanish.

Cultural Variables That May
Affect Assessment and Treatment

Religious and Folk Beliefs

For Hispanics, religious and folk beliefs are similar to those of African American clients (Dana, 1993b; Ho, 1992; R. E. Martinez, 1993; Ruiz, 1988). The priest (for Hispanics who are Catholic) or the minister (for Hispanics with a different religion) are key figures in the process of understanding and assisting Hispanics in solving their problems. Hispanic clients may believe that mental health problems are caused by evil spirits, and, as a result, the church, not the therapist, has the power to treat this problem (Ruiz, 1988). Some Hispanics believe that prayers will cure a physical or mental health problem, and help from a mental health professional may be sought when the family has exhausted all religious and folk belief resources to handle the problem. In addition, some Hispanic believe that certain forms of behavior such as *envidia* (envy) and *mal de ojo* (evil eye), which is said to result from excessive admiration and attention, might result in physical and mental health problems in others. The *espiritista* (spiritistic), *el curandero* (for men) or *la curandera* (for women) (folk healer), and *el brujo* or *la bruja* (witch doctor) can be consulted to resolve these problems. Knowledge concerning these beliefs among the Hispanic communities would enhance the assessment and treatment of Hispanic clients. It is important to emphasize, however, that a therapist should not assume that all Hispanic clients share or are familiar with these beliefs.

Machismo, Respeto, and Marianismo

In general, men tend to be the dominant authority in a Hispanic family, including direct sexual power over women. Qualities that are collectively known as *machismo* include "physical strength," "sexual attractiveness," "masculinity," "aggressiveness," and the ability to consume an excessive amount of alcohol without getting drunk (Comas-Díaz, 1988; Comas-Díaz & Duncan, 1985). Among Hispanic men, machismo also denotes a sense of *respeto* (respect) from others. As noted by Comas-Díaz and Duncan (1985), in general, the term respeto among Hispanics "dictates the appropriate deferential behavior toward others on the basis of age, social position, economic status, and sex" (p. 465). In the context of machismo, the respeto is seen as an example of submission by others (e.g., children and wife) to the authority of a man who believes in machismo. In the context of interpersonal relationships, a Hispanic who shows respeto for the authority (parents, elders, etc.) is considered *una persona bien educada* (a well-educated person). This person has been taught by his or her parents, for example, the importance of demonstrating social relationships *con respeto* (with respect) and *dignidad* (dignity). Therefore, if a child is called *mal educado* (without education), the implicit assumption in the Hispanic community is that this child did not receive education from his or her parents concerning the treatment of others (particularly persons in a position of authority) with respeto. As noted by Ho (1992), in the Hispanic community, an individual "could be illiterate and still be considered *una persona bien educada* [italics added]" (p. 108) if that person has good skills in human relationships and is able to show respeto in the presence of others (particularly, authority such as parents and elders).

Thus, if during the intake process, a Hispanic father reports that "Mi hijo no tienes educacion" (my son does not have education), this statement would mean that his son does not show respeto to him and other people with authority. A therapist unfamiliar with this issue would emphasize a line of questioning dealing with the son's school performances rather than with questions involving further screening of respeto in the current context.

In the case of marianismo (Comas-Díaz, 1988; Comas-Díaz & Duncan, 1985; Martinez, 1988; Ruiz, 1981), women are expected to be submissive, obedient, dependent, timid, docile, sentimental, gentle, and to remain a virgin until marriage. Women are also expected to take care of children at home and to devote their time to cooking, cleaning the house, and doing other activities for the benefit of their children and husband. This marianismo is a phenomenon based on the Catholic worship of the Virgin Mary, who is considered among Hispanics as both a virgin and a madonna (Comas-Díaz & Duncan, 1985). In a general sense, marianismo means that women are not only spiritually superior to men, but also, in the Hispanic communities, they are the individuals who endure all suffering produced by men (Comas-Díaz, 1988; Comas-Díaz & Duncan, 1985).

When Hispanics move from their country of origin (where the distinction between machismo and marianismo is socially accepted) to the United States (where the phenomena of machismo and marianismo are not socially accepted), an attempt to keep the qualities of machismo (in men) and marianismo (in women) may lead to conflicts among family members (e.g., marital problems between husband and wife, and child-father conflicts). In this circumstance, the most practical approach would be to avoid changing those beliefs during psychotherapy and, instead, to present concrete examples leading to the client's understanding of why such beliefs are not socially accepted in the United States.

Familismo

Among Hispanics, the client-family relationship is paramount (Ho, 1992; Ruiz, 1981). Thus, any attempt to conduct psychotherapy without the involvement of the client's family (including nuclear and extended family) is the route to failure. Hispanics generally turn to family members during time of stress and economic difficulties and often consult with other members in the family before they decide to seek help from a therapist. This is particularly true in the case of more traditional Hispanic families compared to more acculturated families (L. Comas-Díaz, personal communication, January 1994). This consultation sometimes involves members from the extended family network who are not related to the family by blood or marriage but are tied to the family through special relationships, such as the godfather (padrino), godmother (madrina), and friends. Role flexibility is not rewarded in the Hispanic communities. The father is the head of the family, the wife takes care of the children, and children must behave according to the father's rules.

Personalismo

In general, Hispanics are more oriented toward people than impersonal relationships (Bernal & Gutierrez, 1988; Ho, 1992; C. Martinez, 1993). This phenomenon is known as *personalismo* (personalism). In general, Hispanics feel uncomfortable when they are treated as "things" or "abstractions." This feeling could include perceiving that the distance between the speaker (e.g., the client) and the listener (e.g., the therapist) is wide, sensing a lack of "warmth" because they are not hugged when they shake hands with someone else (e.g., the therapist), or feeling that someone avoids sharing "personal" information.

Personalismo could indirectly affect Hispanics' selection of the therapist and the process of psychotherapy for this group. For example, many Hispanic clients might select a therapist not on the basis of professional credentials but on the basis of the therapist's ability to self-disclose personal information (excluding intimate aspects of the therapist's life), such as food preferences, music, and hobbies, that enables the client to develop a certain level of trust and confidence in the client-therapist relationship. This observation, however, may not apply in the case of Hispanics with professional status who, in addition to personalism, also tend to look for professional credentials when seeking help from mental health professionals (L. Comas-Díaz, personal communication, January 1994).

Another expression of personalismo during the process of psychotherapy is the offering of gifts or presents by Hispanic clients as a way of expressing gratitude and generosity for the services provided by the therapist. Systematic rejection of such gifts may hurt the client's feeling of personalismo, which in turn could result in the client dropping out of therapy. Therapists working with Hispanic clients, however, need to recognize and acknowledge the conditions in which it is culturally appropriate to accept such gifts (e.g., during Christmas, a Mexican American client gives the therapist a wooden cup made in Mexico) and those conditions in which it may be clinically appropriate to reject the gift (e.g., receiving the wooden cup as a form of payment for therapy).

Individualismo

American individualism emphasizes competition among people, leading to an individual's ability to obtain economic and professional success without the assistance of other members of the community (Sandoval & De La Roza, 1986). In the case of Hispanics, *individualismo* emphasizes what is unique for each member of the community and how this uniqueness leads to cooperation rather than to competition in the Hispanic community (Canino & Canino, 1993). Among Hispanics, individualismo means that everyone has something to offer to the Hispanic community. This offering is the individual's peculiarity that makes him or her unique in comparison to other members of the Hispanic community. This could include, for example, particular job skills and cooking skills.

Among many Hispanics, individualismo and familismo are related in that an individual's own peculiarities are expected to be shared by all members of the family (e.g., mother's ability to cook traditional Hispanic dishes is shared by all family members). The sense of individualismo should be explored in the assessment and treatment of Hispanic clients. This is particularly recommended in those cases in which the client feels or perceives that the therapist's suggestions for changing behaviors means that the client's sense of individualismo could be jeopardized.

Fatalismo

Believing that a divine providence governs the world and that an individual cannot control or prevent adversity is an example of Hispanics' sense of *fatalismo* (fatalism; Ho, 1992; Neff & Hoppe, 1993). Among Hispanics, fatalism might be interpreted in at least two ways. Fatalism could imply a sense of vulnerability and lack of control in the presence of adverse events as well as the feeling that such events are "waiting" to affect the life of the individual. This belief could negatively affect the treatment of Hispanic clients, particularly in those cases in which the goals of therapy compete with the client's perception that no protections exist against problems with a root on fatalism. Fatalism may also be interpreted in terms of an adaptive response to uncontrollable life situations experienced by Hispanics and other diverse groups (Neff & Hoppe, 1993). This sense of fatalism is often associated with the individual's involvement in religious activities, which provide the individual with both personal and social resources. Thus, in the treatment of a fatalistic Hispanic client, it would be important to carefully screen which form of fatalism applies to the client. If the client is fatalistic in accordance with the first form of fatalism, it would be appropriate to encourage that client to get involved in religious activities to minimize the negative impact of fatalism (in the sense of lack of control in the presence of adverse events) during the treatment process (Neff & Hoppe, 1993).

Perception of Skin Color

In the United States, the terms black and white constitute the major racial denomination. Among Hispanics, a wide range of racial denominations exists (Ramos-McKay, Comas-Díaz, & Rivera, 1988). This observation is particularly true in the case of Puerto Ricans, Cubans, and Dominicans. For example, dark-skinned persons are called *morenos* or *prietos,* and those with olive skin or dark complexions are *triguenos.* Persons with light skin or kinky hair are known as *grifos, jabaos,* or *albino*; people having Indian characteristics are called *indio.*

Among many Hispanics, membership in society is much more a function of class (e.g., low socioeconomic status vs. high socioeconomic status) rather than color. Many Hispanics often say that "the green color is the most important color" (i.e., the color of a dollar). Thus, Hispanics with a low socioeconomic status in their country of origin believe that when they are discriminated against in their own country, it is because they belong to a class with little economical resources, regardless of their skin color. When Hispanics enter the United States, however, they experience a different sense of discrimination when they find out that skin color could be an important variable in the phenomenon of discrimination. For example, many morenos or prietos do not classify themselves as black (or African American). When these persons enter the United States, however, they find out that they are perceived as blacks. Because in many Hispanic families some members are morenos or prietos and other members are grifos or jabaos (resembling the white skin color), such families experience an even more dramatic crisis of identity when they find out that some of their members are perceived as blacks and others are treated as whites in the United States.

Because many Hispanics do not emphasize skin colors to make racial classifications, the therapist should avoid traditional race denominations during the process of assessment and treatment of Hispanic clients. The therapist, however, should explore the client's preference of a given skin color in his or her family and how this preference may affect the assessment and treatment of the client. For example, some Hispanic parents (particularly Mexican American parents) would prefer children with light skin color because such parents believe that "if one looks and acts European, one is more acceptable" (Ho, 1992, p. 105). As noted by Ho, darker children raised in a family in which skin color (e.g., light skin vs. dark skin) is more of an issue (with preference given to light-skinned persons) could develop serious self-identity conflicts. A preference by parents in having children with light skin colors might be a function of acculturation (S. Z. Ramirez, personal communication, January 1994). Thus, in the current context, it is also important to conduct an assessment of acculturation (see Table 8.1) and to integrate it in the overall assessment and treatment of the case.

Being Insane Versus Mental Illness

As noted by Dana (1993b), many Hispanics believe a mental disorder (*enfermedad mental*) is less severe than being insane (*estar loco*). In the first case, the person is suffering from a *crisis nerviosa* or *ataque de nervios* (i.e., a nervous crisis). In the second case, the client shows a complete loss of control or withdrawal or both requiring hospitalization (e.g., schizophrenia and major depression). Hispanics who perceive themselves as having a enfermedad mental would seek help from friends, relatives, and healers rather than from mental health professionals. Therefore, when a family member brings his or her Hispanic relative to the clinic, it is important to remember that the family member may consider the client "loco" in the sense that he or she is seriously disturbed.

The First Session

Several specific guidelines have been proposed to facilitate the first encounter between the Hispanic client and the therapist (Bernal & Gutierrez, 1988; Dana, 1993b; Ho, 1992; C. Martinez, 1988, 1993; Ramos-McKay et al., 1988; Ruiz, 1981). A summary of important guidelines in the current context is provided in the following sections.

Explore the Level of Acculturation

An assessment of both internal and external processes of acculturation should always be considered during the first session with all Hispanic clients (Dana, 1993b; Ho, 1992; Norris, Ford, & Bova, 1996; Ramirez, Paniagua, Linskey, & O'Boyle, 1993; Ramirez, Wassef, Paniagua, Linskey, & O'Boyle, 1994). The discrepancy in the degree or level of acculturation among family members may itself produce conflicts in the family leading to "mental problems." This is particularly true in those cases in which the "identified" client is a child or an adolescent (Bernal & Gutierrez, 1988). For example, many traditional Hispanic families believe that a female adolescent must introduce her boyfriend to her parents before dating can be allowed. Dating is sometimes a complex process, including the participation of parents or relatives (e.g., uncles and aunts) in the actual dating. In the United States, this process of dating is not generally accepted by American adolescents. Thus, an acculturated adolescent Hispanic female residing in New York City with a family with traditional (Hispanic) values of what constitutes "dating" would create a "family problem" when she decides to behave in a way different from that expected by her parents when dating a man (see Bernal & Gutierrez, 1988, pp. 250-252, for an illustrative case). In this example, parents may report that their daughter "became very depressed" (including diminished interest or pleasure in most activities, significant weight loss, and suicidal ideation) when she was told that dating will not be allowed without formal approval from her parents. At this point, a therapist with experience with the Hispanic culture would quickly realize that in this specific case, the girl is not meeting her parents' cultural expectations regarding dating. In this example, the girl is considered more acculturated to the American value of dating than are her parents (Martinez, 1986). During this first session, the therapist would probably recommend that such a discrepancy between levels of acculturation among family members be carefully explored before giving advice regarding the solution of that family problem (which could be, in the final analysis, a cultural problem).

Another important traditional Hispanic value is the belief that women cannot have the same freedom and autonomy of men. Thus, a belief in marianismo and machismo is strongly reinforced among many Hispanic families (Comas-Díaz & Duncan, 1985). The process of acculturation, however, may change this belief, and the task of the therapist is to determine how to deal with family problems that appear to be determined by that process of acculturation. If, during the first session, a therapist recommends that a Hispanic wife should have the same freedom and independence as her (Hispanic) husband, this recommendation would be an error (which could lead to attrition) and a sign of lack of understanding of the impact of that particular value on a given Hispanic family.

A guideline to handle the previous examples (and other similar examples indicating the potential effect of acculturation in the manifestation of mental problems) would be to screen the processes of acculturation (as described in Chapter 2) in each member of the family. A summary of acculturation scales recommended with Hispanic clients is included in Chapter 8. In subsequent sessions, the emphasis should be placed on a general discussion involving the concept of acculturation and how the family interprets this concept. In fact, this discussion may serve as one of the basic elements of a treatment plan with emphasis on family therapy.

Formalismo Versus Personalismo

As noted previously, many Hispanics expect personalismo in their relationships with other people, including personal contacts and personal attention. With Hispanic clients, however, personalism should be avoided during the first session and an emphasis on formalismo should be considered. Two strategies are recommended to signal Hispanic clients that proper formal relationships will be considered and respected. The first strategy is to avoid using a first-name informal relationship during the first session. For example, the clinician will say "Good morning, Mr. Garcia" instead of "Hi, Juan" to a Hispanic client who just came for his first session. If the clinician can communicate in Spanish, the form *usted* (formal "you") instead of the form *tu* (informal "you") should be used (Martinez, 1986). For example, during the first session the therapist would say to a Hispanic client, *"Como estas usted?"* ("How are you?") instead of *"Como estas tu?"* Because the word you is used in English to mean both usted and tu, it may be difficult for a clinician to determine in which condition the word you would mean usted rather than tu when communicating in English. The solution to this difficulty is actually very easy to remember: Always use the client's last name and the forms *Mr.* (e.g., Mr. Martinez), *Mrs.* (Mrs. Martinez), or *Miss* (Miss Martinez) before using the form you in the particular sentence. For example, a clinician would say "Mr. Martinez, you said that . . . " instead of "Juan, you said that . . . " In the first case, the meaning of the word you would be usted in the client's interpretation of a formal relationship (which in that sentence is given by the use of the client's last name and the forms Mr., Mrs., or Miss). If the therapist can speak Spanish, it is recommended to address the client as *Señor* (Mr.), *Señora* (Mrs.), or *Señorita* (Miss). Among Hispanics, the term Señor is used with adult males regardless of marital status; the term Señora is generally used to address women who are married. A Señorita is a woman who is at least 15 years old, not married, and considered a *virgen* (i.e., without a history of a sexual relationship with a man).

Other terms used by many Hispanics to identify the status of a family member within the nuclear or extended family are *Don* and *Doña*. Don may be used to identify a Hispanic man with social and economical resources beyond those shared by other members of the Hispanic community. For example, the owner of a farm would be called Don (e.g., Don Martinez). Doña is generally used to identify the wife of that man (e.g., Doña Martinez). In general, however, both terms are used as a sign of *mucho respeto* (very much respect) for elderly Hispanics, regardless of socioeconomic status (e.g., younger members of the Hispanic community would call Mr. and Mrs. Martinez Don and Doña Martinez as a sign of respect, regardless of the socioeconomic resources of Mr. Martinez and Mrs. Martinez in the community).

The second strategy to indicate that proper formal amenities will be considered and respected during the first session with Hispanic clients is to emphasize a formal conversation, which includes the use of the client's last name and the forms Mr., Mrs., and Miss and a content strictly related to the mental disorder mentioned by the client. Thus, the following example is not recommended with a Hispanic client who just arrived for his first session: "Hi, Juan. My understanding is that you feel sad and need help. By the way, Juan, my notes indicate that your birthday was last week. Did you have a good time?" The client may interpret these remarks as informal and unrelated to the main problem. Such remarks, however, are examples of "chatting" (*la platica*) expected by Hispanic clients after the proper formal amenities have been considered and respected (Martinez, 1986).

Explore the Client's Magical
Explanation of Mental Problems

Many Hispanics believe that mental problems might be determined by bad spirits or the effect of witchcraft (hex). These clients also believe that such problems may be resolved with the assistance of the *espiritista* (spirits) or a *curandero(a)* (healer), who may combine expertise in treating these unseen (negative) events with the expertise of mental health professionals (Martinez, 1986). Sometimes, Hispanics do not want to acknowledge in the first session that they believe in spiritualism (L. Comas-Díaz, personal communication, January 1994). During this session, however, the therapist's ability to explore, understand, and accept the client's magical or spiritual explanatory model of mental problems seems crucial for two reasons.

First, exploring, understanding, and accepting the client's magical or spiritual interpretation of mental disorders may enhance the therapeutic relationship needed during the actual process of psychotherapy. Second, during this process, the therapist may use the client's explanatory model to produce positive behavioral changes. For example, it would be appropriate to indicate to a Hispanic client who maintains such beliefs that in subsequent sessions, the therapist will be pleased to invite the espiritista or curandero(a). Because the espiritista and curandero(a) generally conduct their sessions with a group (and rarely with individual cases), this recommendation is particularly important in those cases in which the therapist plans to conduct group therapy with a group of Hispanic clients who share the same beliefs.

As noted by Martinez (1986), if a therapist plans to work with Hispanic clients, it is not only important to understand these beliefs but also, more importantly, the therapist must be "prepared to function within both systems" (p. 80): the folk belief and the scientific systems. An emphasis on the "scientific" explanation of mental problems would probably compete with beliefs among Hispanic clients regarding the role of spirits and the function of the curanderos in the solution to their mental problems (Dana, 1993b; Ho, 1992). If the therapist prefers to deal with the problem "from a purely scientific point," it would be appropriate to refer the client to another practitioner with training (and interest) in the delivery of mental health services to Hispanic clients with emphasis on both systems (see Garza-Treviño, Ruiz, & Venegas-Samuels, 1997, for specific guidelines regarding a cross-cultural curriculum for mental health professionals interested in serving Hispanic clients).

In this discussion, it should be noted that witch doctors or *brujos* (for men) or *brujas* (for women) are not used by Hispanics in the same way they use the curanderos (men) or curanderas (women). In general, brujos or brujas use the power of the devil to resolve problems; curanderos or curanderas use the power of God, in a spiritual sense (I. Cuellar, personal communication, January 1994). This distinction between the brujo(a) and the curandero(a) should be kept in mind when communicating with Hispanic clients.

Interview the Father Alone

When the problem involves family conflicts in which children are considered (by parents) as the center of that problem, it is recommended that the father be interviewed by the therapist alone for a few minutes during the first session. This approach is a recognition of the father's authority by the therapist. Because of the value that Hispanics attach to the father's authority, that brief meeting between the therapist and the father could signal to the family that the therapist is sensitive to cultural variables among Hispanics and that he or she is ready to respect and to support them during the course of therapy. It is important to note, however, that this approach should not be used with an acculturated family to prevent the mother or wife from perceiving that she has been left out in the assessment and treatment of the case (I. Cuellar, personal communication, January 1994). Therefore, an assessment of acculturation is highly recommended before using this particular guideline.

Give the Sense That Medication Could Be Recommended

Many Hispanic clients expect medication during the first session. The therapist must first explore whether the client believes that medication is an important treatment for his or her problem. If it is important and the therapist disagrees with the use of medication, the next step is to discuss the reasons for not using medication. This point must be discussed during the first session. If medication may be used later, the client should be informed about this possibility (Bernal & Gutierrez, 1988; Ramos-McKay et al., 1988).

A Tentative Solution to the Presenting Problem Is Expected

During the first session, Hispanic clients expect a combination of assessment (what is the problem) and treatment (here is what should be done to deal with this problem). Hispanic clients expect some immediate help from the therapist and at least a tentative solution to their problems (Ho, 1992). Thus, at the end of the first session with a Hispanic client, it is important to provide suggestions or recommendations that the client can use to quickly deal with the problem at home. Informing the client at the end of the first session that more information is needed before a therapeutic approach is recommended may lead to attrition (i.e., the client may not return for therapy).

Conducting Psychotherapy

The following guidelines were selected from Comas-Díaz and Duncan (1985), Dana (1993b), Bernal and Gutierrez (1988), Ho (1992), C. Martinez (1986, 1988, 1993), Ramos-McKay et al. (1988), and Ruiz (1981).

Talk About Spiritual Issues

With all forms of therapy, the Hispanic client tends to expect the therapist to talk about "spiritual factors" that could cause emotional problems (including the *susto* [a magical fright], the *mal puesto* [hex], and *mal de ojo* [evil eye]). As noted earlier, during the first session with Hispanic clients their beliefs about spiritual issues and how these beliefs may control the way the clients think and act should be explored. When conducting psychotherapy in subsequent sessions, this information should be used to facilitate the assessment and treatment with Hispanic clients holding these beliefs.

Use More Personalismo and Less Formalismo

During the psychotherapy process, Hispanic clients would expect less formalismo and more personalismo, including proximity, handshaking, and discussion of personal issues by the therapist. Remember, however, that in the first contact with Hispanic clients, personalismo is not generally recommended.

Recommended Modalities of Therapy

Family Therapy

This form of therapy should be considered as the first therapeutic approach with all Hispanic clients. This is particularly important to remember in the assessment and treatment of migrant families. Most Hispanics would prefer this therapy because it reinforces their view of familismo and extended family. Nonblood extended family members (e.g., friends, the *compadre* [cofather] and the *comadre* [comother]) should be expected in family therapy sessions. When the discrepancy in levels of acculturation among family members is relatively high (e.g., as measured with one or more of the acculturation scales listed in Chapter 8), it is important to discuss these levels using examples that each family member can understand. When using these examples, it is important to emphasize that "being acculturated" does not mean a rejection of familism. For example, in the case of the acculturated daughter (cited previously) having family problems because of her (acculturated) approach to dating, the therapist could say to the Hispanic parents,

Mr. and Mrs. Martinez, I understand your concern. It may help, however, if we talk about the way adolescents date in this country and how this way of dating does not mean that a female adolescent like your daughter is not really concerned about her family.

Traditional values among Hispanic families and new values acquired by later generations (e.g., children of recent immigrant Hispanic parents) should be discussed during family therapy.

Group Therapy

Group therapy is recommended with Hispanic clients, but it should emphasize a problem-focus approach. In addition, several guidelines are often recommended in the literature that should be considered prior to the scheduling of group therapy with Hispanic clients (Martinez, 1986).

If the therapist is bilingual and decides to conduct group therapy in Spanish, it is important to remember that although the grammar of Spanish is generally shared by countries in which the native and official language is Spanish (e.g., Puerto Rico, Cuba, Dominican Republic, and Mexico), many variants in the ways Spanish-speaking people use Spanish in daily conversations can be identified. Thus, clients must be told that although group therapy will be conducted in Spanish, in some cases, it will be necessary for the speaker to explain the meaning of a word, phrase, or sentence that appears difficult to understand by the other members of the group.

A client should not be included in that (Spanish-speaking) group simply because he or she is Hispanic (Martinez, 1986). Acculturated Hispanics may have problems understanding Spanish simply because they do not use their native language or have not used it for a long time. Thus, it is important to screen the level of acculturation to determine the impact that language would have on some members of the group (see Figure 2.1).

Clients sharing the same level of acculturation should be included in the same group (Martinez, 1986). Mixing acculturated clients with nonacculturated clients may lead to major discrepancies regarding the handling of the particular problem under discussion on the basis of differences in values or beliefs among group members. For example, traditional values regarding dating, the role of the mother, the impact of machismo (maleness and virility), and so on shared by recent Hispanic immigrants may conflict with the view of more acculturated Hispanics in group therapy. The Brief Acculturation Scale described in Chapter 2 could be helpful in screening Hispanic clients prior to inclusion of these clients in a given group therapy session.

A therapist involved in group therapy (and other forms of therapy) with Hispanic clients should master the pronunciation of Spanish names. As noted by Martinez (1986), when the therapist pronounces Spanish names correctly, this simple event may indicate to Hispanic clients that the therapist is interested and concerned with their problems. One way to follow this guideline is to practice the Spanish names before the first group therapy session. The question, "How do you say your first and last name?" (*Como usted pronuncia su nombre y su apedillo?*) is not recommended during the first group therapy session.

All members in the group should have the sense that a great amount of flexibility will be allowed by the therapist, particularly in the areas of punctuality and attendance (Martınez, 1986). As noted by Sue and Sue (1990), the therapist should be aware that many Hispanic clients emphasize the event (e.g., social contacts with friends before attending a therapy session) rather than the clock (the assumption that clients should be "on time" or show up early for group therapy). This point should also be remembered during the programming of other interventions with Hispanic clients (e.g., family therapy).

Behavioral Approaches

Behavioral approaches (e.g., behavior therapy, cognitive-behavior therapy, and applied behavior analysis; Paniagua & Baer, 1981) are characterized by their emphasis on the experimental (empirical) analysis of the effect of behavioral interventions in the production of behavioral changes and the assessment of these changes using reliable measures. These approaches, however, do not emphasize the potential impact of race and ethnicity during the assessment and treatment of problem behaviors. The overall assumption in these approaches is that the effectiveness of behavioral interventions would be generalized across people regardless of race or ethnic background. Systematic desensitization and social skills training are examples of empirically tested behavioral interventions recommended in the treatment of Hispanic clients (Jenkins & Ramsey, 1991). Despite empirical findings regarding the effectiveness of these techniques, if they are used with Hispanic clients, the following guidelines should be remembered. The goal of systematic desensitization is to eliminate anxiety occurring in the presence of certain environmental events (Paniagua & Baer, 1981). The effectiveness of this treatment may be facilitated if the therapist uses Hispanic scenes (e.g., "Imagine that you are in a Mexican restaurant") and a Spanish accent (Jenkins & Ramsey, 1991).

Teaching clients to be assertive by using appropriate social skills is the main goal of social skills training (Lange & Jakubowski, 1976). In the absence of an attention on cultural variables, this technique may be inappropriate in those cases in which the goal of intervention is to teach family members, for example, to deal with conflicts between an adolescent and parents, conflicts between husband and wife associated with the wife's intention to be assertive, and other situations in which the authority of the father or husband cannot be questioned. The value that Hispanics place on respeto, machismo marianismo, and familismo are examples of major cultural variables that might discourage assertive behaviors in both Hispanic males and females (Comas-Díaz & Duncan, 1985; Soto, 1983). For example, in many traditional Hispanic families, children and adolescents are not allowed to argue with their parents, and respect toward the father is expected. In this case, teaching assertive behaviors to manage family conflicts involving an adolescent and his or her parents (e.g., saying to a Hispanic father, "You don't want me to date Juan, but I will date him anyway") may be seen as a violation of a fundamental cultural value among Hispanics—namely, that properly respectful behavior toward the Hispanic father is expected by all members of the family, including his children and his wife.

Similarly, a Hispanic female with a belief in marianismo and machismo would not feel comfortable (and might drop out of therapy) with a therapist interested in teaching her assertive behaviors toward her husband (e.g., "You should tell your husband what you exactly think about him. You should be able to express your feelings openly" or "Today, I will teach you how to reject orders from your husband"). Comas-Díaz and Duncan (1985) recommend teaching assertive behaviors to Hispanic clients with an emphasis on a recognition of the authority of the father, husband, and so on before expressing assertive behaviors in a given context. For example, instead of teaching a woman how to reject orders from her husband, a better approach would be to teach her to use certain words that acknowledge the authority of the husband (e.g., "With all the respect that you deserve, I feel/believe . . ." Comas-Díaz & Duncan, 1985, p. 469). This statement places emphasis on the respect toward the husband, which is then followed by the expression of assertive behaviors (e.g., ". . . that I would prefer to visit my family this week").

Medication

Some therapists do not like to use medication for two reasons. First, they do not believe in the effect of drug therapy in the treatment of mental health problems. Second, if they do believe in the therapeutic effects of medication, therapists who are not physicians (e.g., psychologists and social workers) have to depend on the schedule and treatment regimen of a physician (e.g., a psychiatrist). In the treatment of Hispanic clients, however, a key guideline to remember is that many such clients expect medication for the treatment of their mental problems. This is particularly true in the case of Mexican

American clients (Martinez, 1986). If medication is not mentioned during the process of psychotherapy, a Hispanic client may assume that the therapist is not a "good healer," and he or she may not return for subsequent therapy sessions.

If a Hispanic client expects medication for the treatment of his or her mental problem (keep in mind that some Hispanics may not want medication), do not forget that a large set of empirical data exists indicating that certain drugs may be effective in the management (not necessarily treatment) of certain mental problems, such as the use of tricyclic antidepressants in the management of depression (Joyce & Paykel, 1989). This is particularly true in the case of the use of these antidepressants with the four culturally diverse clients described in this book (Silver, Poland, & Lin, 1993).

Regardless of disagreements on the use of medication (in terms of the previous two reasons), recommending empirically tested drugs with clients who are expecting them during the therapy process may result in a "placebo effect" (i.e., the medication is not actually effective, but the client thinks that it is really effective). If this effect actually works with a Hispanic client, it would be beneficial for the client (e.g., the mental problem is less severe over time), and the therapist may claim that he or she was sensitive to the client's cultural expectation regarding the use of medication as a fundamental approach (in the client's mind) in the treatment of the problem. Therefore, if you are treating Hispanic clients and you do not want to recommend medication, you may wish to try it anyway for reasons just mentioned.

If medication is used to manage mental disorders, the following additional guidelines are suggested:

1. The therapist should ask the client directly about his or her expectancy for the prescription of medication to manage (or "cure" in the mind of the client) the problem.

2. If the therapist is not a medical doctor, he or she should consult with an adult or a child psychiatrist (they have more training and expertise in this area in comparison with general physicians) regarding the most appropriate medication for the target mental disorder.

3. The therapist should develop a checklist to screen the possibility of short-term and long-term side effects and discuss these effects with the client each time he or she returns to the clinic. If side effects are reported by the client, the therapist should discuss them with the person prescribing the medication.

4. The therapist should keep in mind that medication will not cure the mental disorder; it might help in the management of the disorder.

5. The therapist should be aware of the tendency to rely exclusively on medication and ignore other aspects of therapy.

Music Therapy and *Cuento* Therapy

A Hispanic client may feel uncomfortable discussing a problem with the therapist. With this client, music therapy may be recommended to assist him or her in dealing indirectly with the main problem. The *plena* is recommended to communicate current events, the *salsa* emphasizes the struggle for survival, and the *bolero* states the nature of relationships. *Cuento therapy* (storytelling) is recommended for those children who prefer to talk about their problems with the assistance of readings by the therapist and interpretation of the readings by the children.

**Avoid Insight-Oriented and
Rational-Emotive Therapies**

In general, insight-oriented psychotherapy emphasizes internal conflicts and blames the client for his or her own problems. Many Hispanics believe that problems in their life emerge because of external conflicts with the environment, and other people should be blamed for their problems. Rational-emotive therapy is an argumentative or logistical talking therapy or both that competes with the cultural phenomenon of machismo shared by many Hispanic families.

5

Guidelines for the Assessment
and Treatment of Asian Clients

The third largest multicultural group in mental health services in the United States is the Asians. In general, the Asians comprise three major subgroups (Mollica, 1989; Mollica & Lavelle, 1988; Sue & Sue, 1990): Asian Americans (Japanese, Chinese, Filipinos, Asian Indians, and Koreans), Asian Pacific Islanders (Hawaiians, Samoans, and Guamanians), and Southeast Asian refugees (Vietnamese, Cambodians, and Laotians). In 1995, the Asian population in the United States (all three groups) was 9.66 million (U.S. Bureau of the Census, 1996).

Among Asians, the most numerous groups in the 1990 U.S. Census (Kim, McLeod, & Shantzis, 1992) were the Chinese (812,000), Filipinos (782,000), and the Japanese (716,000). The majority of Asians live in urban areas, particularly in California, Texas, and Washington State. In 1995, the median income for Asians was $46,106, which was higher than both the national average ($39,276) and the average income level of whites ($40,884; U.S. Bureau of the Census, 1996). In 1995, the incomes of 13.1% of Asian families and 14.6% of Asian persons were below the poverty line (U.S. Bureau of the Census, 1996).

Among Asians, the Southeast Asian refugees are the most disadvantaged. For example, in summarizing the median income for Asians in 1980, Kim et al.

(1992) reported a median income for the Vietnamese of $12,840, whereas the median income for the Asian Americans and the Pacific Islanders ranged from $20,459 to $27,657 and $14,242 to $19,196, respectively (in 1980, the Japanese had the highest median income, i.e., $27,354, and the Samoans had the lowest median income, i.e., $14,242). In 1980, the U.S. population median income was $19,917. In addition, in 1980, the income level of 35.1% of Vietnamese was below the poverty line (Kim et al., 1992) in comparison with much lower overall mean percentages below the poverty level as reported by Asian American subgroups (8.6%) and Pacific Islander subgroups (17.8%; Kim et al., 1992).

Cultural Variables That May
Affect Assessment and Treatment

Prejudice, Racism, and Discrimination

Prejudice, racism, and discrimination have historically been reported among Asians living in the United States (Sue & Sue, 1990; Yamamoto, 1986). This is particularly true during the immigration of Chinese to the United States in the 1850s through World War II to work in the gold mines and on the railroads. The Chinese were followed by other Asians (Japanese, Filipinos, Koreans, etc.). Asian men who immigrated to the United States as a source of cheap labor during that period were considered "sneaky and sinister" and were prohibited from owning American land or bringing their wives with them. Discrimination was also apparent in housing, employment, and educational opportunities (Yamamoto, 1986). Yamamoto has noted that despite significant improvement in the life of Asians in the United States, "prejudice, racism, and discrimination still persist" in this group (p. 92). Thus, non-Asian therapists should be sensitive to these historical events among Asians in the United States and avoid verbal and nonverbal behaviors that could be interpreted by Asian clients as signs of prejudice, racism, or discrimination during the therapist-client therapeutic relationship.

Familism

Asians also place great emphasis on the individual-family relationship (Ho, 1992; Sue & Sue, 1990). Among Asians, the family is first and then the individual. American individualism is not rewarded, and, like the Hispanics, Asians view individualism as an example of the individual's peculiarities. Like the Hispanic and African American families, Asians also place great emphasis on the extended family. Among Asians, however, the role for each family member must be very clear and cannot be changed. Like the Hispanic families, the role of the father is to function as the dominant figure in the family, and his authority is paramount. In addition, the sense of "role flexibility" generally seen among African Americans is not emphasized among Asian Americans.

Role of Children and Wives

Among traditional Asians, the primary duty of children is to be good and to respect their parents. Parents can determine children's personal desires and ambition, and any attempt not to comply with parents' expectations is seen as a threat toward the parents' authority. Asian women are expected to marry, be obedient, be helpers, have children, and to respect the authority of the father. This may explain why Asian women and children appear less autonomous and assertive and more conforming, dependent, inhibited, and obedient to authority in comparison with Anglo women and children (Ho, 1992; Sue & Sue, 1990). These are appropriate (or normal) behavior patterns among Asians. A therapist who considers the independence of an individual from his or her family as an example of autonomy and assertiveness in that individual would interpret these behavior patterns among Asians as inappropriate. A therapist familiar with these behavior patterns among Asians, however, would avoid giving suggestions to an Asian family with emphasis on the independence of children and adolescents from the authority of their parents. This therapist would also avoid a discussion regarding the lack of assertive behaviors and autonomy in Asian women during the process of family therapy.

Public Suppression of Problems

In general, Asians do not encourage members of the group to publicly express their problems to other people outside the group (Sue & Sue, 1990). All problems (including physical and mental problems) must be shared only among family members, just as all credits and successes received by an individual must also be shared by the entire family. Shame and guilt are mechanisms used by Asian families to enforce norms in the family (Dana, 1993b). These mechanisms play a crucial role in preventing Asians from reporting or admitting their problems in public.

If an Asian does not show the behaviors expected within and outside the family, he or she may lose confidence and support from the family, which could lead to the development of a strong sense of shame and guilt in that person. This sense of shame and guilt may lead to considerable anxiety and depression regarding the feeling and thought that family support may be withdrawn. Several Asian scholars (e.g., Ho, 1992; Sue & Sue, 1990) have noted that this sense of shame and guilt among Asians may explain the strong self-control and self-discipline often reported among Asians. Thus, an important guideline is to explore this sense of shame and guilt among Asian clients to understand how difficult it is for these clients to talk about their problems in public. Because of this normative and cultural approach to shame and guilt, a therapist should not expect that an Asian client will report about his or her emotional problems as soon as the request "Tell me about your problems" is presented (just as it is generally the case with many African American and Hispanic clients who tend to quickly respond to this question the first time they interact with the therapist).

Indirect Versus Direct Forms of Communication

When Asians are exposed to verbal communication, they often look quiet and passive, make a great deal of effort to avoid offending others, sometimes answer all questions affirmatively to be polite when they cannot understand the therapist's questions, and avoid eye contact (Chung, 1992; Root, Ho, & Sue, 1986). This form of verbal communication is indirect, and it is very appropriate among Asian Americans. This communication pattern, however, is different from the direct form of verbal communication based on Western standards of communication in which both the speaker (e.g., the client) and the listener (e.g., the therapist) must look expressive and active, and generally do not answer questions that cannot be understood.

Silence and lack of eye contact are forms of indirect communication that may create problems during the assessment and treatment of Asian clients. Among Asians, silence is a sign of respect, politeness, and a desire to continue speaking after making a point during a conversation (Sue & Sue, 1990).

Eye contact during direct verbal communication is expected in the Western culture because it implies attention and respect toward others. Among Asians, however, eye contact is considered a sign of lack of respect and attention, particularly to the authority (e.g., parents) and older people. A therapist without understanding of the use of silence and lack of eye contact by Asians may feel uncomfortable and may change the entire content of the conversation on the assumption that the client is not interested in the particular point or is not attending to what the therapist is saying. This tactic may prevent many Asian clients from either elaborating on a prior point or demonstrating an acceptable form of attention and respect (e.g., through silence and lack of eye contact) toward the listener (i.e., the therapist).

The First Session

Expertise and Authority

Many Asian clients come to their first therapy session believing that the therapist will tell them what is wrong and how to resolve their problems (Sue & Sue, 1990). In addition, in the minds of many Asian clients the therapist is the authority. The therapist, then, must demonstrate these two qualities (i.e., expertise and authority) during the first session to ensure that the client will return to the clinic. Kim (1985) suggested the following practical guidelines to assist Asian clients in their recognition of the expertise and authority of the therapist during the first session:

1. Casually mention prior experiences with other clients with similar problems. For example, the therapist could say, "In my experience with many similar cases . . ." (to show expertise) or "In my professional judgment . . . " (to show authority).
2. Display diplomas, licenses, and books.
3. Use professional title when introducing yourself to the client (e.g., "I am Doctor . . . " or "I am Professor . . . ").
4. Provide possible reasons or explanations for the "cause" of the problem.
5. Give the impression that a tentative solution (cure) to the problem is possible.
6. Throughout the first session, emphasize concrete and tangible goals and avoid comments suggesting that you will see the client for a long period of time (for Asian clients, only inexperienced doctors need a lot of time to understand and resolve a problem).

Maintain Formalism and Conversational Distance

In general, Asians tend to perceive the therapist as the "authority," and they feel that their role is to be passive, respectful, and obedient in the presence of the therapist (Yamamoto, 1986). Thus, formalism in the therapist-client relationship is expected among Asian clients. Do not expect that the client will be too friendly during the first meeting. The initial contact between the therapist and an Asian client is generally formal. Jokes should be avoided during this session. The nature of the relationship often determines the conversational distance between an Asian and other people. The basic guideline is to allow the client to define that distance during the process of assessment and treatment. For example, the therapist would sit first and allow the Asian client to determine the conversational distance. If a trusting relationship between the Asian client and the therapist is not yet built, the client would not sit close to the therapist (Chung, 1992).

Do Not Expect an Open or
Public Discussion of Emotional Problems

An individual's emotional problems bring shame and guilt to the Asian family, preventing any family member from reporting such problems to others outside the family. This phenomenon probably explains why the prevalence of emotional disorders among Asian clients seems very low in current epidemiological data involving mental disorders across multicultural groups (Sue & Sue, 1990). In the first session with an Asian client, the therapist must show (both verbally and nonverbally) that he or she will wait until the client is ready to discuss mental problems in public. This waiting period could include more than one session, and the Asian client should sense this possibility.

Expect Expression of
Mental Problems in Somatic Terms

Asians tend to express psychological disorders in somatic terms (Ho, 1992; Hughes, 1993; Sue & Sue, 1990). This phenomenon is associated with the shame, humiliation, and guilt that could result from making these problems public (Hughes, 1993). Given the choice of talking about physical symptoms (e.g., chest pains, headaches, and fatigue) or talking about psychiatric symptoms (e.g., hallucinations and delusions), an Asian client would probably select the first choice because physical complaints are often more acceptable (i.e., result in less shame, humiliation, and guilt) than reports about emotional or psychiatric problems in Asian communities (Sue & Sue, 1990).

Thus, when an Asian client consults with a therapist for the first time, he or she would spend a great deal of time talking about physical (medical) complications such as headaches, back pain, weight loss, fatigue, and so on. Two guidelines are recommended (Ho, 1992; Sue & Sue, 1990) to handle Asian clients' somatization of psychological or psychiatric disorders during the first session. First, the therapist should always acknowledge these somatic complaints. He or she should also tell the client that medical consultations (particularly with an Asian physician) for the clinical assessment of potential physical disorders will be arranged before the therapist concludes that the client is exhibiting some form of somatization disorder (e.g., conversion disorder, hypochondriasis, and somatoform pain disorder). Second, the therapist should gradually introduce statements that allow the client to move from verbalizations of somatic complaints to verbalizations involving mental health problems. For example, the therapist could say, "I will consult with a physician for your headaches. Perhaps you are having headaches because you do not know what to do to handle some conflicts in your life. Would you like to talk about these conflicts?" The therapist should avoid statements that indicate that the therapist does not believe that the client really has a physical (medical) problem. The statement, "You don't have headaches. You simply want to avoid talking about your mental problems," is not recommended.

Consider the First Session a Crisis

Because many Asian families believe that mental illness can bring shame and humiliation to the entire family, these families often refuse to seek professional mental help and tend to wait for many years (usually for 5 to 10 years) before seeking such help (Fujii, Fukushima, & Yamamoto, 1993; Gaw, 1993b). Thus, when the client is brought to the attention of a clinician, family members are often in a state of crisis because of their inability to handle a case that has developed into a chronic and severe condition over time. For this reason, the first meeting should always be considered a potential crisis. Because of the possibility of crisis or emergency, the clinician should be prepared to display two emergency responses:

1. Immediate assessment of suicide attempts and thoughts
2. Immediate attention to the presenting problem and its treatment (including the availability of family's supports, possibility of brief inpatient treatment, and consultation with social agencies involved with the Asian communities)

In the second case, the therapist should inform the family whether the client needs brief psychotherapy, inpatient treatment, medication, or all three before the termination of the first session. Yamamoto (1986) pointed out that these guidelines are particularly important for elderly Asians referred to outpatient mental health clinics because of the high frequency of suicidal behavior (approximately 27 in 100,000) among this group living in the United States, whereas the frequency of this behavior is extremely low among elderly Asians living in their countries of origin.

Avoid Discussing Hospitalization

Although it is appropriate to consider the first meeting with an Asian client as a potential crisis situation, it is also important to avoid comments regarding the hospitalization of the client. Many Asian clients consider hospitalization as the last resort and expect to hear about alternatives to psychiatric hospitalization (e.g., outpatient treatment and the delivery of treatments by family members at home) during the first meeting. If the hospitalization of an Asian client is necessary during the first meeting (e.g., because the client is a danger to himself or herself or others), the following guidelines should be followed (Fujii et al., 1993; Kinzie & Leung, 1993):

1. Family members must be consulted and approve the hospitalization.
2. Family members and the client must receive a detailed description of the length of stay, recommended tests, and treatment modality.
3. Family members should be told about the number of visiting hours and the reason why having a family member in the hospital with the client is not encouraged (e.g., for clinical or administrative reasons).
4. Family members should be told that they may bring their inpatient relative ethnic foods to replace or supplement Western-style foods offered in the hospital to all inpatients.
5. During the entire period of hospitalization, the client should never be told about his or her diagnosis. Only the family and the therapist should share this information. Many Asians believe that if the client knows "the truth about the illness, he or she might lose hope and deteriorate more quickly" (Fujii et al., 1993, p. 337).

Consider Alternative Care Services

It is a good tactic with Asian clients to assume that the current problem is a chronic problem developed over a long period. Despite the severity of the clinical case, however, many Asian families may not agree with the hospitalization of their relatives. Therefore, prior to the actual contact with an Asian client, it is important to determine the availability of alternative care services. For example, instead of hospitalization, it would be more acceptable (by an Asian family) to consider a discussion (with the client and his or her family) regarding the availability of care of the client at home with some professional assistance. A listing of mental health community services for Asians should also be available during the first session. The following examples of alternatives could facilitate assessment and treatment of Asian families who refuse the hospitalization of a relative to avoid the stigma of mental illness resulting from hospitalization or inpatient treatment (Yamamoto, 1986, p. 117):

1. Asian Community Service Center in Los Angeles
2. Pacific and Asian Preventive Program in San Diego

3. The Richmond Area Multi-Service Center in San Francisco

4. The Asian Counseling and Referral Service in Seattle

5. Asian American Drug Abuse Program in Los Angeles

6. The Center for Southeast Asian Refugee Resettlement in San Francisco

7. Asian Counseling and Treatment Center in Los Angeles

8. Korean American Mental Health Service Center in Los Angeles

9. Operation Samahan in San Diego (specializing in outpatient health care for Filipino clients)

Provide Concrete and Tangible Advice

Asian clients want the therapist to deal with their immediate concerns by providing concrete and tangible advice (Root et al., 1986). Prolonged verbal exchanges between the client and the therapist should be avoided. Suggestions that appear ambiguous should also be avoided during this session. For example, the statement, "Mr. Sue, you need to change your behavior in a positive way if you want your wife to stay with you," tells nothing about exactly what Mr. Sue must do. In addition, solutions to problems involving long-range goals should not be discussed during the first session. For example, the following statement is both ambiguous and implies a long-term goal: "Let's talk about what you need to do to change your behavior in the next six months. What do you think you should do to improve your relationship with your wife?" A better statement with an Asian client would be, "During the next five days, write on a piece of paper the number of times you and your wife hold hands, eat, and take short walks together. When you return for therapy next week, we will talk about what you wrote." This statement is concrete (i.e., it tells the client exactly what to do to improve the relationship), and it suggests a short-term goal (i.e., the task assigned to the client will be discussed the following week).

Psychotherapy Is Not Expected

During the first session, Asian clients would expect that the therapist wants to know about the client "in general." Conducting psychotherapy to deal with the client's problem is not expected during the first session (and in some cases, several sessions would be necessary before psychotherapy can actually be initiated). As noted previously, if the therapist determines that he or she is dealing with an emergency situation or crisis, the use of inpatient treatment or medication or both should be considered.

In general, however, an Asian client would not expect the use of psychotherapy (or other forms of intervention) during the first session. As noted previously, the public admission of problems (particularly mental problems) is not encouraged among Asians. Thus, the therapist cannot expect that during the first session, the Asian client will share his or her feelings and emotional problems with someone outside his or her immediate family (Sue & Sue, 1990). The best approach would be to give a sense that the therapist is "here" to listen and that the therapist understands that it may take several sessions before the client agrees to discuss emotional problems openly.

Consider the Client's Organic Explanation of Emotional Problems

Because Asian clients tend to express their emotional problems in somatic terms (Sue & Sue, 1990), these clients generally place a great deal of emphasis on the explanation of their emotional problems in terms of organic variables. For this reason, Asian clients expect medication (to deal with these "organic" problems) during their first contact with the therapist. A practical guideline recommended in this specific case is to accept the client's own interpretation of the origin of his or her mental problems as an example of the client's belief system. This tactic could greatly enhance the therapist-client relationship in future sessions. If medication will not be recommended during the first session, the therapist should also discuss the reason for not prescribing medication in concrete terms. For example, with Asian clients the statement, "I don't think you need medication," is ambiguous because the client still needs to know why medication will not be prescribed. A better statement would be the following:

> To improve communication between you and your wife, I would like to recommend a technique based on learning how to solve problems. Medication is another alternative, which I might consider later after consulting with your physician regarding the medication you are currently taking to prevent complications by combining two or more medications.

Do Not Try to Know Everything During the First Meeting

In general, during the first meeting with the client, practitioners have been trained to conduct a "thorough" clinical interview (getting as much information as possible during the meeting). This approach is not recommended with Asian clients (Gaw, 1993b). Questions dealing with specific and sensitive issues (e.g., "How is your sexual relationship with your wife?") should be avoided, and more general statements are suggested (e.g., "How is the relationship between you and your wife?"). Emphasis on general statements could enhance the therapist-client therapeutic relationship during the first session and prepares the road for questioning the client about intimate matters in subsequent sessions.

Southeast Asian Refugee Clients

The previous guidelines are suggested with all Asian clients. The following guidelines are strongly recommended with Southeast Asian refugee clients (Cook & Timberlake, 1989; Mollica, 1989; Mollica & Lavelle, 1988). As noted previously, Southeast Asian refugee clients come to the United States with a history of traumatic events generally not reported by other Asian clients (particularly Asian American and Pacific Islanders clients). For this reason, the first session with a Southeast Asian refugee client should be planned carefully. The following sections provide examples of specific points to consider with this group (Ho, 1992; Mollica & Lavelle 1988).

Avoid Questions Dealing With Traumatic Events

During the first session with this group, it is extremely important to avoid statements, questions, commentaries, and so on dealing with traumatic events. It is important to be familiar with the fact that these clients come to therapy with a history of torture, killing of loved ones, missing family members, witnessed killing, sexual abuse acts experienced by women and children during the war, and so on. It would be extremely difficult for the patient to openly discuss these events during his or her first meeting with the therapist. Because of the long history of traumatic events among Southeast Asian refugees, the client should not leave the clinic without an assessment of suicide attempts, organic brain syndrome (because of potential head injury), and depression.

Do Not Encourage the Client to Say
More Than What He or She Wants to Say

Encouraging a Southeast Asian refugee to talk about his or her problems during the first session could be very stressful for the client. Thus, these clients should not be encouraged to say more than what they are actually saying at the present moment. For example, the statements, "Are you sure that this is the reason why you need help?" and "Do you think that some dreams about very bad events in your life are creating problems for you?" should always be avoided during the first session.

Give a Sense That Stress Will
Reduce as Quickly as Possible

These clients expect help from the therapist in terms of providing quick solutions to their level of stress caused by a lack of resources to afford housing, food, clothing, and other vital elements for their survival in the United States (Cook & Timberlake, 1989). In this case, the therapist should be familiar with social services (particularly agencies specifically created to deal with refugees) in the community that could assist the clients with their needs to minimize the level of stress.

Conducting Psychotherapy

The guidelines presented in this section are recommended when conducting psychotherapy with Asians. The guidelines were selected from Chung (1992), Ho (1992), Mollica and Lavelle (1988), Murase (1992), Root et al. (1986), Sue and Sue (1990), and Yamamoto (1986).

Psychoeducation of Asian Clients

Because many Asian clients do not understand terms such as therapy, psychotherapy, verbal therapy, psychodynamic therapy, and behavior therapy and how these therapies differ from traditional (healing) methods, it is necessary to begin the psychotherapy process with a brief discussion regarding the meaning of such terms (Kim, 1993).

Conduct an Assessment of Shame and Humiliation

During the process of psychotherapy with Asian clients, it is important to conduct an assessment of the persistence of shame and humiliation resulting from the stigma of mental illness and to discuss this issue with the client and family members. After the first meeting (which is often a crisis situation), an assessment of the persistence of shame and humiliation could include attention to the following points (Gaw, 1993b), which a therapist may use to infer that the client is having a problem talking openly about mental problems because of the shame and humiliation resulting from the public admission of such problems:

1. The client or a family member is extremely concerned about the qualification of the therapist.
2. The client is excessively worried about confidentiality.
3. The client refuses to cover expenses with private insurance.
4. The client has difficulty in keeping appointments or frequently arrives late for therapy.
5. Family members refuse to support the use of treatment.
6. The client insists on receiving services from an Anglo clinician to avoid Asian therapists.
7. The client refuses to seek treatment even in those cases in which a severe mental health problem is evident.

Discuss the Duration of Therapy

Most Asians expect a quick solution to their mental problems. As noted previously, however, Asians often seek professional help for chronic psychiatric disorders. Asian clients should be informed that a quick solution to chronic mental health problems is unrealistic, and they should be informed about the approximate duration of treatment (Yamamoto, Silva, Justice, Chang, & Leong, 1993). Long-term treatment periods with emphasis on the uncovering of underlying conflicts are not recommended with Asian clients (Murase, 1992). Short-term treatment periods are recommended, which should not be longer than 2 or 3 months. An extension of these short-term treatment periods must be negotiated with the client.

Avoid Personalism

Compared to the Hispanics, Asian clients do not expect "personalism" during psychotherapy; a formal relationship with the client during the first session is expected to continue in subsequent sessions.

Recommended Modalities of Therapies

Medication

Medication is expected by many Asian clients. Drug dosages recommended for Anglo clients, however, cannot automatically be prescribed for Asian clients because of "differences in body weight and possible ethnic differences in drug metabolism and sensitivities" (Gaw, 1993b, p. 276). If medication is used with Asians, the overall recommendation is to use low doses because of the tendency of these clients to respond to much lower doses in comparison with non-Asian clients (Fujii et al., 1993; Kinzie & Leung, 1993). Because many Asian clients use herbal medications to treat physical and mental problems, a discussion of potential side effects resulting from the consumption of traditional medicines in combination with the client's compliance with psychotropic medication is recommended.

Behavioral Approaches

Behavioral approaches (e.g., behavior therapy techniques) are recommended with Asian clients because they are concrete and directive and do not emphasize the exploration of internal conflicts leading to enhancement of the "shame" that the client experiences by reporting his or her problems.

Family Therapy

When working with Asian clients, the programming of family therapy is recommended for two reasons (Berg & Jaya, 1993). First, among Asians, the family (as a unit) is more important than the individual. Second, the word privacy (in the sense of withholding information among family members) is foreign to many Asians (Hughes, 1993; Sue & Sue, 1990). Thus, an Asian client would expect his or her family to be actively involved in the assessment and treatment of the case, and the therapist would be expected to share information regarding assessment and treatment issues with all family members (not only with the client). Additional guidelines in the programming of family therapy with Asian clients include the following (Berg & Jaya, 1993):

1. Problem-solving techniques used to deal with marital problems and conflict between children and parents among Asian clients should emphasize a process of negotiation rather than a process of head-on confrontation. In this process of negotiation, the therapist is seen as the mediator, who is expected to be an expert in a position of authority.

2. To enhance a peaceful negotiation, the client or the parties in conflict should be seen separately before the family members are seen together in family therapy sessions.

3. Consider the differences in age and status when addressing family members. For example, the head of the family (e.g., the father) should always be addressed first using his or her last name and any title (e.g., Mr. Sue, Doctor Sue, and Mrs. Sue). During the therapy process, an Asian client may ask the

therapist to call him or her by the first name; until this request is evident, the therapist should show proper and formal relationships with the client. As noted by Berg and Jaya (1993), many Asian clients believe that the respect they receive from a therapist is often more important than what the therapist does to help them solve their problems.

4. Family therapy must be (a) problem focused, (b) goal oriented, and (c) symptom relieving on a short-term basis (Kim, 1985). Emphasis on internal conflicts, self-assertion, expression of anger, and acquisition of insights as goals in family therapy is not recommended with Asian American clients (Kim, 1985). Such clients would expect a therapist to define the goals of family therapy in terms of situational changes requiring external solution.

5. Because of the expected parental authoritative role by children toward their parents (Ho, 1987), the programming of family therapy leading to the development of the independence of Asian children and adolescents from their parents is not recommended. In their social contacts with American children, however, Asian American children quickly learn that in the typical American parenting style, democracy is emphasized within the family in which children are allowed to speak, question authority, and are encouraged to be independent. If family therapy is recommended with Asian families, this sharing of power among family members in the Western culture may compete with the vertical, hierarchical structure of Asian families in which parents (particularly the father) are in a position of unquestionable authority (Kim, 1985). Thus, before the scheduling of family therapy with an Asian family, the therapist must determine whether all family members in therapy share the same value concerning the expected undisputable leadership and authority of parents. In this process, an evaluation of the level of acculturation among family members is recommended (see discussion on acculturation in Chapters 2 and 8).

6. Because Asians emphasize the family first (and the individual second), relationship questions are recommended during the process of assessment and treatment (Berg & Jaya, 1993). For example, the following questions do not emphasize a relationship between the client and other family members: "What do you think about your problem?" "If you stop drinking after treatment, how would you feel?" and "How does this problem affect you?" The same questions, however, can be phrased in terms of a relationship between the client and other family members. For example, "What do you think your father will say is the main problem between you and him?" "If you stop drinking after treatment, what will your family notice you doing differently?" and "How does this problem affect your family?"

7. Always avoid embarrassing the family members in front of each other. The therapist should always protect the dignity and self-respect of the client and his or her family. This guideline is often termed "saving face" (Berg & Jaya, 1993; Kim, 1993). For example, an Asian father would "lose face" during the process of family therapy if he is told by the therapist (in the presence of other family members) that he is "wrong" in demanding that the son cannot select a

profession that is unacceptable to his parents. To avoid embarrassing the father in the presence of his son, the therapist would compliment the father and reframe the issue in a positive way. For example, "I understand that you would like your son to have a profession that could help the family's financial situation. But would you agree that your son would be happier if he selects a profession that is rewarding to him *and* to the family?" In this case, the therapist would preserve the dignity and proper role of the father ("face saving") and provide an alternative solution to the problem (i.e., allowing the son and his parents to make a compromised decision regarding the selection of the son's profession).

8. If the central issue in family therapy is divorce, the following practical guidelines are recommended (Ho, 1987). First, because divorce is not socially acceptable among the Asian communities and it is seen as a very important decision by family members, a practitioner should not provide the idea of divorce as an alternative, and instead, he or she should wait until the client clearly indicates that it is time to discuss this alternative. Second, many Asian clients are not familiar with legal divorce proceedings, and the task for the practitioner would be to provide the client with legal information and with the name, address, and phone number of lawyers with knowledge and expertise regarding the client's cultural background. Third, relatives and close friends may feel that the client's decision to divorce could bring shame to the entire family, which may lead to the withdrawal of social and economic supports from these relatives and friends. The practitioner's role is to assist the client to find a new support system by encouraging the client to meet other Asian divorcées who share the same experiences. This third guideline may be implemented through the scheduling of group therapy involving Asian clients sharing similar experiences.

9. The overall assumption is that Asian clients would prefer to involve the entire family in the assessment and treatment of their mental disorders. This assumption, however, must be carefully evaluated with each Asian client. As noted by Yamamoto (1986), acculturated Asian clients may or may not want family members involved in psychotherapy. Thus, despite the assumption that family ties are paramount among many Asians, it is important to avoid a recommendation of family therapy on the basis of this assumption only. A careful assessment of acculturation is recommended during the application of this guideline (see Table 8.1 for examples of acculturation scales recommended with Asians).

Avoid Talking Therapy

Talking therapy is not recommended with Asian clients. For many Asian clients, active therapy (i.e., doing something to quickly deal with the problem) has more value than "talking cure" (Gaw, 1993b). As noted by Tsui (1985,

p. 360), Asian clients "expect tangible evidence of intervention, not abstract discussion." For this reason, therapies based on self-exploration and psychodynamic interpretations of symptoms are considered to be ineffective with Asian clients.

Select Group Therapy Carefully

Because of their tendency to avoid sharing their problems with people outside the immediate family, group therapy with Asian American clients is not generally recommended. This guideline is particularly relevant in the treatment of Asian clients involving sensitive issues such as sexual dysfunction and infertility (Tsui, 1985). Group therapy, however, would be appropriate in those cases in which the client's support system (relatives and close friends) is not available and an alternative support system is quickly needed. For example, as noted previously, Asian clients who elect to divorce and do not receive support from their relatives and close friends could share their experiences with other Asian clients who also were neglected by their family and friends because of a similar "misbehavior" (i.e., the divorce; see Ho, 1987, p. 63).

Additional Guidelines for Southeast Asian Refugee Clients

In addition to the previous guidelines recommended for all Asian clients, during the process of psychotherapy, three specific guidelines are suggested with Southeast Asian refugee clients. First, despite the role of the extended family, a discussion of the potential use of family therapy should be considered carefully because the family may not be available (e.g., deaths in the family during wars).

Second, during the process of psychotherapy, the therapist should be ready to assist the client in the pursuit of three categories of services (Flaskerud & Anh, 1988). During the community and education services, the therapist would provide information to the client regarding mental health centers as resources for treatment, education about mental disorders, and education about American society (including culture and lifestyle). In the case of social services, a refugee should be informed about financial assistance, community resources for food and housing, and vocational and language training opportunities in the community. In the provision of social services, the client should be informed about culturally relevant assessment and treatment for mental disorders, family-related problems, and adjustment problems.

Third, recent reports indicate that approximately 50% of Southeast Asian refugees in the general population could be suffering from posttraumatic stress disorder (PTSD; Kinzie & Leung (1993). Therefore, after the first contact with a Southeast Asian refugee client the psychotherapy process in subsequent sessions should include a thorough screening for PTSD and discussions of specific stressful events responsible for this disorder. The therapist, however, should keep in mind that the client may not discuss feelings involving traumatic experiences for many months because the client does not voluntarily reveal severe traumas during the initial evaluation, the primary symptoms for PTSD (e.g., recurrent distressing dreams, bad irritability) are not generally mentioned by the client during the first meeting because he or she thinks that the symptoms are unrelated to the presenting problem, or because many refugees simply avoid talking about traumatic events under any situation. In addition, a Southeast Asian refugee might not talk about these events because he or she realizes that the clinician does not want to listen "to the terrible stories and the agony endured by the refugees" (Kinzie & Leung, 1993, p. 290).

Social Skills Training for
Southeast Asian Refugees

Social skills training is particularly recommended for Asian refugee immigrants with severe fear of deportation or fear that they may give a bad reputation to other Asians because of their assertive behaviors (Yamamoto et al., 1993).

6

Guidelines for the Assessment and
Treatment of American Indian Clients

The American Indian population is the fourth major multicultural group in
mental health services in the United States (Thompson, Walker, & Silk-
Walker, 1993). The American Indian population is also known as Native
Americans, but this term is not recommended because it does not include
other Indian groups in the United States (e.g., Eskimos and Aleuts) and
Indians from other countries (e.g., Canadian and Mexican Indians) that have
settled in the United States (Fleming, 1992). The preferred terms are American Indians and Alaska Natives (Fleming, 1992; Thompson et al., 1993).
Thompson et al. (1993, p. 189) suggested that the term Indian should be used
to "refer to all American Indian, Alaska Natives, and Canadian and Mexican
Indian people." In terms of the assessment and treatment of Indians in the
continental United States, the American Indians constitute the most common
Indians seen in mental health services (Ho, 1992; Richardson, 1981). In
addition, historical analyses involving the precontact period (i.e., the time
before the North American continent was "discovered" by Europeans in
1492) and subsequent periods had emphasized American Indians (Walker &
LaDue, 1986). Thus, the majority of historical and clinical materials reported
in this chapter are representative of American Indians.

In 1995, the American Indian (all groups) population was 2.2 million (U.S. Bureau of the Census, 1996). The majority of American Indians currently live in six states: Alaska, Arizona, California, Oklahoma, New Mexico, and Washington State (U.S. Bureau of the Census, 1996). Approximately 339,836 American Indians live on 278 federal and state reservations, and most reservations have fewer than 1,000 Indians (Ho, 1992). In 1995, the median income for the American Indian families was $21,619 (U.S. Bureau of the Census, 1996). The estimation for Indians living in reservations is much lower (approximately $9,942; Ho, 1992). In 1995, the income level of 31.2% of American Indians families was below the poverty level in comparison with those of 9.1% white families and 11.7% white persons below the poverty level (U.S. Bureau of the Census, 1996). Among the four groups discussed in this text, the American Indians are currently the most disadvantaged in terms of socioeconomic characteristics, mortality, and life expectancy (Kim et al., 1992; U.S. Department of Health and Human Services, 1991).

Is the Client an Authentic Indian?

If an American Indian wants to be considered for assistance from federal Indian programs, he or she must prove his or her status as an "Indian" in terms of the definition established by the Bureau of Indian Affairs, housed in the U.S. Department of the Interior (Ho, 1992; Jaimes, 1996; Sue & Sue, 1990; Trimble & Fleming, 1989; Wise & Miller, 1983). This definition states that the client must have at least one-quarter Indian "blood" and a proof of tribal status (Harjo, 1993; Ho, 1987; Jaimes, 1996). It is important to note, however, that the federal government is not the final word on the definition; the federal government must recognize the sovereign status of each tribal definition of Indian (A. McDonald, personal communication, January 1994; O'Brien, 1989). Because it is extremely difficult to apply this definition in clinical practices, practitioners should seek consultation from Indian organizations (see Table 6.1) and tribal leaders in those cases in which the assistance of federal Indian programs is necessary to manage the case but the client is not sure of his or her Indian status at the moment of contact with the mental health agency. The worst approach is to ask the client, "Are you sure that you meet the definition of an Indian in this country?" The reason why this is not a good question in clinical practice is that many American Indians considered the blood quantum formula "pseudoscientific . . . and it is still viewed as racist by many Indians" (Jaimes, 1996, p. 50).

Cultural Variables That May
Affect Assessment and Treatment

Historical Events and Their
Impact on Mental Health Services

Walker and LaDue (1986) suggest that practitioners who want to assess and treat American Indians should be familiar with critical events during four time intervals and the impact of these events on American Indian clients. These time intervals are (a) the precontact period (prior to 1492), (b) the Manifest Destiny period (1492-1890), (c) the assimilation period (1890-1970), and (d) the Indian self-determination period (1970 to the present).

Precontact Period

Many of today's rules, roles, values, beliefs, and so on among American Indians were developed during the precontact period. An important element in that period is termed the "survival pact," which included the rules that govern the "symbiotic relationship among the individual, the group, and the earth. . . . [These rules] touched all aspects of life, including marriage and social encounters, food gathering, hunting and fishing, religion, and medicine. . . . As long as tribes followed these rules, they survived and prospered" (Walker & LaDue, 1986, p. 145). These features of the survival pact have passed from generation to generation by ways of legends, histories, and songs.

A recent example of what could happen to the individual or the group if the survival pact is violated is the "mystery illness" (a flu-like illness that provoked acute respiratory distress and deaths) experienced by the Navajo Nation in 1993 and the explanation of the origin of this illness by many Navajos. According to reports published in the *Houston Chronicle,* a Navajo reported that "the tribal elders . . . feel that the disease is a prophecy of Mother Earth. . . . The medicine men are saying [the illness occurred] because of something we have done wrong, for not taking better care of the Earth" (Foreman, 1993, p. 18A). Later, health officials from New Mexico reported that the mystery illness was caused by the Hanta virus, which is present in rodent droppings and urine. On the basis of this information, Western doctors consulted with the medicine men in an effort to minimize fears and deal with the disease. This example not only illustrates the function of the survival pact among American Indians (exemplified here with America's largest Indian tribe, i.e., the Navajo Nation) but also shows the role that the medicine men currently play in a moment of crisis and the attention and respect they receive from the scientific community (familiar with the role of the medicine men among American Indians).

Manifest Destiny Period

Two important events during this period (1492-1890) were the impact of epidemics on the lives of many Indian people and the development of racism and discrimination with the creation of the reservations and the boarding schools. A familiarity with both events could help practitioners to understand why many American Indian clients do not trust Anglo mental health professionals. Diseases such as smallpox, cholera, malaria, pneumonia, syphilis, diphtheria, and typhoid fever are generally considered examples of "European diseases" that early explorers (white men from other lands) introduced in the lands of the American Indians (Brandon, 1989; Walker & LaDue, 1986). These diseases produced massive numbers of deaths among the Indians. A consequence of the devastating effect of such epidemics was a drastic change in many of the features of the survival pact. For example, prior to the epidemics, the job of the medicine man was to cure all diseases regardless of their causes. European diseases, however, were not examples of "Indian diseases" that the medicine man was able to cure. Thus, the medicine man was "of little practical or spiritual value to his tribe" (Walker & LaDue, 1986, p. 153). In addition, the epidemics killed many of the elders and tribal leaders who taught the rules of the survival pact (e.g., the harmony between the group and the earth as a measure of stability in the tribe, beliefs in supernatural and spiritual events, and values and rules of behavior). These events led to the loss of the meaning of the survival pact in the minds of many American Indians, which, prior to the epidemics was considered a critical element in their lives. The European diseases not only contributed to the loss of many features of the survival pact but also led to the conversion to Christianity. Walker and LaDue (1986) suggested that this conversion occurred for two reasons. First, the epidemics left little hope among the Indians for a "return to the traditional ways" (p. 156). Second, "the Christian promise of a better afterlife must have seemed quite inviting" (p. 156). It is now clear, however, that the role of the Christian religion during such epidemics was to impose Christian beliefs and rules of conduct for the tribes, including the elimination of all cultural values of the survival pact.

The creation of reservations was initially considered by American Indians as a positive event in their struggle to move away from the influence of whites on their lives, culture, language, and religion (Walker & LaDue, 1986). Thus, tribes were relocated in areas remote from white settlement called reservations. American Indians were promised vast amounts of land and protection from the influences of whites. These promises, however, were broken many times, including the reduction in lands and relocation of tribes; elimination of existing reservations; the introduction of legislation making the language, religion, and customs of Indians illegal; and the exiling of tribal leaders. These events "make reservations unhappy and miserable" (Walker & LaDue, 1986, p. 157). Another negative event in that time was the creation of the boarding schools by the government and various (non-Indian) religious groups (Reyhner & Eder, 1988). The main goal of these schools was to replace the practice of Indian language, dress, beliefs, religion, and customs with the practice of the white civilization. In such schools, Indian "children were punished severely for speaking their own language . . . [and the message was that] to be Indian was to be bad" (Walker & LaDue, 1986, p. 157).

Assimilation Period

This period (1890-1970) served to reinforce the development of racism and discrimination experienced by American Indians during the creation of the reservations and boarding schools (O'Brien, 1989). During the early years of the assimilation period, Indians had two choices: death or the assimilation of the white culture. Many Indians moved away from their old traditions not only to avoid death but also as a result of the deaths of the Great Chiefs, who were instrumental in the transmission of such traditions to their people (Walker & LaDue, 1986). Despite these negative events in the lives of many Indians, during the assimilation period, old traditions among tribes continued and two important victories occurred in the lives of American Indians: Indians became the last people in this country to receive full citizenship and voting privileges, and the Indian Reorganization Act was passed, which, among other things, gave the American Indians the right to govern their people using traditional values and their own culture (O'Brien, 1989). These victories, however, were followed in the 1950s by another attempt by whites to force Indians to assimilate (accept and practice) the standards of the white society. These attempts are called termination and relocation (Jaimes, 1996; Walker & LaDue, 1986). The termination involved the elimination of all special agreements and relationships between the federal government and the tribes. The relocation consisted of moving American Indians living on reservations into urban cities. These measures led to increases in already existing social (e.g., cultural ambivalence) and behavior (e.g., depression and alcoholism) problems among Indians, but white men again failed to eliminate the Indian culture and old values.

Self-Determination Period

This period (1970 to the present) is characterized by an increase in the number of Indians in leadership roles in federal Indian programs and four congressional acts to benefit the Indians (Goodluck, 1993; O'Brien, 1989; Walker & LaDue, 1986): the Indian Self-Determination Act (1975), Indian Health Care Improvement Act (1976), Indian Child Welfare Act (1978), and the Indian Religious Freedom Act (1978). These are, of course, positive events in the history of American Indians. It is, however, very difficult for this group to forget the treatment that they received from whites and to believe that a period of termination or relocation will not come again. Thus, American Indians are still very suspicious of white people and tend to mistrust anyone outside their society (particularly whites) who makes promises to them concerning socioeconomic, political, and cultural opportunities outside their own lands. Mental health professionals interested in working with American Indian clients should be familiar with the overall effects of the historical events in the lives of American Indians. This guideline is particularly relevant for white mental health professionals who, during the process of assessment and treatment, may feel that they are being "rejected" or "mistrusted" by an American Indian client without apparent reasons.

The Indian Child Welfare Act. Practitioners involved in the assessment and treatment of Indian children must have "extensive knowledge of the Indian Child Welfare Act [ICWA; passed by the U.S. Congress in 1978] and its implications for the client system" (Goodluck, 1993, p. 222). This act "acknowledged the tribe as *the best agency to determine custody* [italics added] issues for Indian children. The Act reaffirmed that tribes *possessed jurisdiction over child-custody proceedings* [italics added] for all Indian children living on the reservation" (O'Brien, 1989, p. 212). In addition, the ICWA states that if an Indian child resides off reservation or in a Public Law 280 state (a state with the authority to use its civil and criminal laws on reservations), the state court is required to transfer jurisdiction to the tribal court unless the parents object to this requirement (O'Brien, 1989). Thus, a therapist should not handle court actions involving child abuse, foster care, and adoption among American Indian families in the absence of extensive knowledge and applicability of the ICWA. The following are the basic elements of this act (Goodluck, 1993):

- Child custody proceedings (e.g., procedures for defining a child as Indian, tribal court jurisdiction, placement standards, and returning of the child to tribal jurisdiction)

- Indian child and family program development (provides information for tribes interested in developing service programs for Indian children)
- Record keeping and information (e.g., procedures for disclosure of information and Indians' rights and benefits)

Familism

Like the African Americans, Hispanics, and Asians, among the American Indians, the extended family has primacy; the self is secondary. The self (individual) is also secondary with respect to the role of the tribe (Richardson, 1981). The family and the group take precedence over the individual. In comparison to Hispanics and Asians, the emphasis is placed on the "administration" of the family by the father and older relatives rather than on "authority" (Asians) or machismo (Hispanics). Thus, mutual respect between wife and husband, between parents and children, between family members and relatives, and between family members and the tribe is highly rewarded (Ho, 1992; Matheson, 1986; Richardson, 1981).

A strong family relationship is emphasized, but a sense of independence among family members is rewarded, particularly among American Indian children and adolescents (Ho, 1992). For example, American Indian children are rarely told directly what to do and are often encouraged to make their own decision. Among American Indians, few rules are best, and if they exist, they must be flexible and loosely written (Richardson, 1981). This cultural value includes the administration of the family and children by parents, relatives, and tribe leaders. During the assessment and treatment of American Indians, it is particularly important to avoid looking for the "head" of the family with the authority to make decisions regarding the entire family. Contrary to the Asians' and Hispanics' fathers, among American Indian families, the father (or older adults) only administers the family; he does not control the family in the sense of being "authoritarian" or "macho."

An important cultural value among American Indians' perception of familism is the consultation of tribal leaders, the elderly, and the medicine man or woman when marital conflicts emerge. This is particularly important in those cases in which husband and wife are from two different tribes (e.g., Cherokee vs. Hopi tribes) and the main conflict involves the discipline of their children. If the therapist suspects that such conflicts may be the result of different values, norms, and beliefs between tribes, an elder from either tribe should be consulted to clarify cultural differences between the two tribes and the contribution of such differences in the manifestation of these conflicts.

Sharing and the Concept of Time

Everything must be shared among American Indians, including the solution to problems, material goods, and time (Ho, 1992). American Indians treat time as a natural event and do not believe that time should control their natural way of living (Ho, 1992). Time among many American Indians is not used as a measuring tool (i.e., hours, minutes, etc.), but rather, it is related to holistic task (A. McDonald, personal communication, January 1994). That is, the event (task) rather than the clock is what is important among many American Indians. (Sue & Sue, 1990, p. 128, suggested that a similar concept of time may be held by many Hispanics, for which the task or event has primacy over time.) In the same way that material goods must be shared, many American Indians believe that time (to fulfill a given task) must also be shared with others. For example, an American Indian client may be late for his or her therapy session not because he or she wants to be late or is resistant to the therapy but because, on the way to the clinic, the client met a friend and spent time talking about family matters, business, or other issues. In this example, the task (e.g., the client's social contact with that friend) is more important than punctuality (i.e., the clock). Therefore, questioning this particular client for the reasons for being late is a bad strategy and a sign that the therapist is not familiar with the way time is used by American Indians.

Nonverbal Communication

Like the Asians, American Indians also place great emphasis on nonverbal forms of communication. Among American Indians, listening is more important than talking (Matheson, 1986; Richardson, 1981). A belief among American Indians is that one can learn a great deal just by listening to what other people are saying. Thus, American Indians will communicate feelings and emotions through clues with their bodies, eyes, and tone of voice. An American Indian client who looks "quiet" during the therapy session is actually listening and attending very carefully to the therapist's verbal remarks. Similarly, when the client is talking, he or she expects the therapist to listen and to carefully attend to both verbal and nonverbal cues from the client. When the client perceives that the therapist is listening, this perception is translated into a recognition that the therapist understands the problem and that he or she may have good suggestions for the solution of that problem.

Two special forms of nonverbal communication are lack of eye contact and slight handshake. In the Western culture, eye contact is a sign of respect and attention to others. For many American Indians, however, eye contact is a sign of disrespect. Thus, "forcing" an American Indian client to look directly at the eyes of the therapist could make the client very uncomfortable (Thompson et al., 1993). As noted by Johnson, Fenton, Kracht, Weiner, and Guggenheim (1988), American Indians generally pass hands with a slight touch and believe that a firm handshake represents a sign of aggression. Failure to appreciate this cultural distinctiveness may lead to error in the diagnosis of many American Indian clients. For example, an American Indian client who avoids eye contact, firm handshake, and generally shows other nonverbal communication styles considered in the Western culture as *psychomotor retardation* could easily be diagnosed with depression (Johnson et al., 1988).

Individualism

Like Hispanic and Asian clients, American Indians reject the traditional sense of individualism leading to competition among family members and between American Indians and other people (Richardson, 1981). American Indians may be seen as "unmotivated," "lazy," and "unproductive" because they do not share the American individualism. Among American Indians, the emphasis is on collectivism and the sense of "working together" to achieve common goals among all members of the tribe; a recognition of the qualities of the individual and his or her independence, however, is also emphasized (O'Brien, 1989). Thus, therapists need to understand the implicit harmony between the rights of an individual self-actualization versus tribal's actualization or survival or both (A. McDonald, personal communication, January 1994). A failure to recognize the implicit harmony between individualism and collectivism among many American Indians could lead to failures in the assessment and treatment of this group. For example, if, during the process of psychotherapy, an American Indian client believes that the therapist is recommending a procedure or technique that may lead to discord and disharmony among family and tribal members, that client will not follow through with the recommendation (Sue & Sue, 1990).

The First Session

Recognize Limited Understanding of American Indians' Culture and the Positive Feeling of Being an Indian

If the therapist is not an American Indian, he or she should begin the first session with a clear statement regarding the therapist's limited understanding regarding cultural values, religions, and traditions among American Indians. The therapist should also verbally state that he or she would like the client to correct any error or offensive statement based on the therapist's lack of understanding of the client's culture and values (Richardson, 1981). In addition, during this session, it is appropriate to let American Indian clients know that their history shows that they are good people and that they should feel proud of themselves.

Avoid Pseudosecrecy Statements and Do Not Ask
Questions Unrelated to the Core Clinical Problem

The therapist should avoid statements such as "Feel free to tell me . . ." or "You can rest assured I will not discuss your problems with . . ." As noted by Richardson (1981) and Walker and LaDue (1986), Indians have heard these statements many times from the Great White Father and the federal bureaucrats, and each time they have been deceived. Similarly, questions unrelated with the core problems should be avoided. For example, it may not be appropriate to ask an American Indian client, "What does your father think about the restriction on hunting?" or "Why don't Indians share the same tradition in the management of children across tribes?" These questions would be considered offensive to American Indians (Richardson, 1981).

Do Not Discuss Medication

During the first meeting, it is particularly important for the therapist to avoid statements regarding the use of medication to treat the problem. Many Indians believe that synthetic medication is not good for the health of Indians (Thompson et al., 1993).

Accept Relatives, Friends, Medicine Man
or Woman, and Tribal Leader

If the client brings unexpected people during the first meeting, do not be surprised. American Indians do not mind sharing their emotional problems with their relatives, friends, tribal leader, and the medicine man or woman (Richardson, 1981).

Avoid Taking Many Notes

An American Indian client wants you to listen, and taking notes is a sign of not listening and disrespect. Taking notes makes the process of the interview more formal and structured, which is the opposite of American Indians' beliefs in simplicity and flexibility during their social contacts with other people (Ho, 1987; Richardson, 1981). If you have to take notes, it is important to ask permission from the client, and remember to summarize these notes at the end of the session to indicate that you understood the main concern rather than simply took notes. If you sense that taking notes is not allowed (through nonverbal signals from the client), then show the client (nonverbally) that it is acceptable not to take notes.

Listening Rather Than Talking

Many American Indian clients come to see the therapist because they want the therapist to listen to what they have to say about the core clinical problem; these clients do not come to therapy to listen to the therapist. Thus, it is important that the therapist use his or her "ears" rather than his or her "mouth" during the first session with an Indian client.

Confidentiality Versus Resistance

During the first session, an American Indian client from a small Indian community may not want to answer questions dealing with his or her personal or private life. This attitude may be erroneously considered a case of resistance from the client and mistrust toward the therapist. The client, however, is aware that relatives and friends may work in the hospital or clinic and will not answer such questions for fear that his or her answers will be entered in the medical record and become public (Thompson et al., 1993). Thus, after an overall statement concerning confidentiality (which is always recommended with clients from all multicultural groups) if the client refuses to answer such questions, the appropriate approach is not to label the client's behavior as "resistance" but to consider it as a sign indicating that issues of confidentiality have not been resolved. The second approach is to directly ask the client if he or she is aware of relatives or friends working in that hospital or clinic. If the answer is affirmative, the client should be allowed to make his or her own decision regarding the best way to handle the situation. Making a promise to an American Indian client regarding the maintenance of confidentiality may be a bad tactic. Only the client would know whether such relatives and friends should be trusted.

Explore Important Potential Problems

During the first session with American Indian clients, particular attention should be placed on the screening of alcoholism and depression symptoms. Alcoholism is not only the primary concern among American Indians but also has been considered to be the main cause of suicide and violence in this group (Choney, Berryhill-Paapke, & Robbins, 1995; O'Brien, 1989; Walker & LaDue, 1986). It is also important to screen Indian women for symptoms of alcoholism to prevent fetal alcohol syndrome (a disease that produces severe physical, social, and intellectual deficits among children of alcoholic women). Feelings of inadequacy and low self-esteem are indications of depression in this group. These feelings have been associated with the negative impact of the reservations and the Indian boarding schools (Walker & LaDue, 1986). In addition, stress and other emotional problems are often associated with relocation (i.e., moving out of the reservations and relocating in urban areas). Therefore, it is important to determine whether or not the client recently moved from the reservation. In subsequent sessions, an American Indian client who sees himself or herself affected by these events would benefit from discussing these events with practitioners who can understand the development of such events and their dramatic effects on the lives of American Indians, particularly during the manifest destiny and assimilation historical periods described previously.

Conducting Psychotherapy

Traditional Healers and Mental Health Professionals

The use of traditional healers (e.g., the medicine man or woman) in the interpretation and solution of problems among American Indians is increasing among Indians living in urban areas and reservations (Choney et al., 1995; Matheson, 1986; Richardson, 1981; Walker & LaDue, 1986). Thus, many American Indian clients seeking professional help for their mental health disorders will expect the professional to be familiar with and ready to integrate traditional healing practices with Western healing practices.

A list of legitimate healers could greatly enhance the process of the therapist's credibility (as described in Chapter 2). This list may be obtained from local Indian boards and specialized institutions such as the Dull Knife Memorial College, a tribal college founded on the northern Cheyenne reservation in 1979 (see Table 6.1). In fact, it is recommended that clinicians (in particular, non-Indian practitioners) encourage an American Indian client to consult traditional healers in the Indian communities and to discuss with the therapist ways to integrate Western and traditional healers during the course of assessment and treatment (Thompson et al., 1993). (It is important to emphasize that although Indian healers often practice healing to control evil spirits, these healers do not generally practice black magic or witchcraft, i.e., the use of the healing process to harm others [Thompson et al., 1993].)

Finally, Thompson et al. (1993) suggest that it would be inappropriate to question American Indians about details involving specific procedures used by Indian healers. Thompson et al. note that many American Indians believe that if those procedures "are to be revealed at all to non-Indians, or even to someone from another tribe, it is only after a long and trusting relationship has been established" (p. 208).

Recommended Modalities of Therapies

The following are guidelines recommended for all forms of psychotherapy conducted with American Indian clients (Ho, 1987, 1992; Thompson et al., 1993; Walker & LaDue, 1986):

1. For many Indians, the present is more important than the future. In this case, the practitioner should be able to quickly screen this perception of time to determine whether therapy should be oriented toward the present.

2. Many American Indians believe that it is disrespectful to ask many questions, and when American Indians ask questions during the process of psychotherapy, the function of such questions is to clarify instructions given by the therapist.

3. Basic survival issues and unmet needs in the particular American Indian family or client under treatment should be explored by using a nondirective approach. Moving from the reservation into urban areas, unemployment, medical complications, and poverty are examples of survival issues and unmet needs that may lead to violence, heavy drinking, and marital problems.

4. Once the potential impact of survival issues and unmet needs has been explored, a directive problem-solving and social skill training approach is recommended in which the therapist suggests a concrete and feasible solution to problems. The assistance of the medicine man or woman may be combined with the problem-solving and social skills training approach.

5. Many American Indian clients expect from mental health professionals some clarification concerning the cause(s) of their problems and what exactly they can do to deal with such problems. This expectation requires considerable time and flexibility from the therapist.

6. For American Indian clients who travel a great distance for therapy, it is important to have a plan that may be offered to the client to encourage subsequent visits to the clinic and facilitate the effects of treatment. The following points should be considered in that plan (Thompson et al., 1993): use of self-help groups close to the client's residence; recruitment of the healthiest members of the family as "cotherapists" (who can be instructed to assist with the use and monitoring of the therapist's instructions at home); and use of brief therapy with short-term objectives.

Behavioral Approaches

These approaches are recommended for American Indian clients because they emphasize the cause of behavior (including maladaptive behavior) as determined primarily by external events and avoid explanation of behavior in terms of internal conflicts (Walker & LaDue, 1986). An important element in the behavioral approaches shared by American Indians is the emphasis on environmental events leading to disruptions in one important aspect of the survival pact: the symbiotic relationship between the environment and the individual or the group. Similarly, many American Indians believe that problems in the individual and the group can result from a disruptive individual- or group-environment relationship caused by the effects of negative events in their lives (e.g., epidemics, the creation of reservations, and Indian boarding schools). Behavioral approaches teach clients how to establish better relationships with the environment by making viable decisions in the presence of external (negative) events and by modifying external behavior-consequence relationships leading to changes in behavior (Walker & LaDue, 1986).

Family Therapy

Many American Indian families believe that the reason that the client is experiencing a family problem (e.g., marital problems, difficulties in handling their children, and school problems) is that the family does not have the ability to provide essential needs to their members, including food, shelter, and health (Ho, 1987). Thus, if family therapy is recommended with this group, it is important to initially deal with the family's basic needs, including the provision of concrete advice regarding the fulfillment of these needs. It is recommended to have available a listing of social agencies specializing in American Indians and to discuss this list with the family. This approach would show that the therapist is sensitive to the family's basic needs and that he or she is able to provide immediate delivery of concrete services, which in turn could lead to the enhancement of a trusting family-therapy therapeutic relationship.

During the entire family therapy process, additional guidelines include the following (Ho, 1987):

1. The therapist should emphasize group decision by involving all nuclear and extended family members (including the medicine man or woman and tribal leaders).
2. All suggestions given to the family should be presented in a concrete, slow, and calm mode, which would indicate that the therapist is sensitive to flexibility in the time-oriented approach among American Indians.

3. The therapist should determine the tribal identity of the family and whether all members involved in the family belong to the same tribe. As noted earlier, this guideline is particularly important in those cases in which the family's problems involve conflicts between husband and wife regarding the management of their children. For example, in the Hopi tribe, the wife is primarily responsible for the management of children, whereas in the Cherokee tribe, the disciplining of children is shared by both husband and wife. Thus, a Cherokee woman who marries a Hopi man would express marital discord with her husband if he shows no concerns regarding the discipline of their children (Ho, 1992, pp. 154-155).

4. The therapist should allow family members to decide what exactly they want to manage during the process of family therapy. For example, an American Indian family would come to family therapy to seek help with how to fulfill some basic needs. When these needs are fulfilled, that family would terminate therapy (Ho, 1987). If the same family returns for additional family therapy sessions (after those basic needs have been achieved), this is a sign that family members believe that it is time to deal with relationship problems and reasons for the initial contact to the clinic. These reasons could include marital problems, school difficulties among Indian children and adolescents, alcoholism, and so on (Ho, 1987).

Group Therapy

A common belief is that group therapy is not appropriate for American Indians. Several scholars, however, believe that this observation is not totally true. For example, Arthur McDonald (personal communication, January 1994), Manson, Walker, and Kivlahan (1987), and Thompson et al. (1993) recommend the use of group therapy with American Indian clients (particularly in the prevention and management of alcoholism), especially when it is programmed in combination with traditional Indian activities. In addition, Manson et al. (1987) pointed out that it is appropriate to recommend group therapy with American Indian clients because this intervention "is an outgrowth of the natural emphasis on groups in the social ecology of most Indian and Native communities" (p. 170). The following three specific guidelines should be remembered when group therapy is programmed with American Indian clients (Sue & Sue, 1990; Thompson et al., 1993):

1. Support or permission or both from tribal officials should be obtained before scheduling group therapy.

2. If the therapist is not an Indian, he or she should conduct group therapy with the assistance of Indian professionals (e.g., Indian social workers, teachers, school counselors, psychologists, and psychiatrists).

3. The medicine man or woman, tribal leaders, elders, and other respected tribal members should be invited to participate actively in some group therapy sessions (members of the group should be consulted regarding the applicability of this recommendation and who may provide suggestions to determine the selection of tribal members with high status in the tribe).

Medication

The use of medication in the treatment of mental disorders among Indian people has not been systematically studied or reviewed. Thompson et al. (1993), however, noted that most classes of psychotropic medication are effective with this group. Remember, however, that during the first meeting with an American Indian client, discussions involving the possibility of drug therapy should be avoided.

Psychodynamic Model

For many American Indians, mental problems are the result of external events rather than the result of internal conflicts or difficulties with the personality of the individual. In general, psychodynamic psychotherapy does not take into account environmental events and places heavy emphasis on internal conflicts. Thus, this approach is not recommended with American Indian clients (Walker & LaDue, 1986).

Treatment of Children

Regardless of the kind of treatment used, if an Indian child is the target client, the most important guideline to remember is to avoid giving recommendations to parents that appear to indicate that an Indian child is being forced to behave or not to behave in a certain way. A "rightness of choice" (Ho, 1987, p. 77) is expected among Indian children, and the main task of parents is to assist their children in making the right choice. Thus, a treatment plan with emphasis on ordering, verbal reprimands, and threat is not recommended in the management of Indian children.

Foster Care and Adoption

Before making decisions regarding the placement of Indian children in foster care or adoption, it is important to remember that the Indian Child Welfare Act provides that Indian families must have preference in making

TABLE 6.1 Organizations for American Indians

Association on American Indian Affairs
432 Park Avenue South, New York, NY 10016
(212) 689-8720

Dull Knife Memorial College
P.O. Box 98, Lame Deer, MT 39040
(406) 477-6219

National Indian Social Worker's Association
1740 West 41st Street, Tulsa, OK 74107
(505) 446-8432

Northwest Indian Child Welfare Association
Box 751, Portland, OR 97207
(503) 725-3038

The Indian Family Circle Project
New Mexico Department of Social Services
P.O. Box Drawer 5160, Santa Fe, NM 87502
(505) 827-8400

Urban Indian Child Resource Center
390 Euclid Avenue, Oakland, CA 94610
(510) 356-2121

that decision. That is, a clinician should not make decisions regarding foster care and adoption without consultation with the tribe and parents (O'Brien, 1989; Thompson et al., 1993). This guideline is particularly important to remember in those cases in which such decisions include the placement of Indian children with non-Indian families.

Organizations for American Indians

Because of the number of policies and regulations (some from the government and others from the tribes) among American Indian communities, it is important to consult with organizations specialized with these communities to enhance the process of assessment and treatment of American Indian clients. Examples of these organizations are listed in Table 6.1. Readers interested in a quick reference regarding these policies and regulations across Indian tribes are encouraged to consult the book *American Indian Tribal Governments* (O'Brien, 1989).

7

Guidelines for the Prevention of
Attrition of African American,
American Indian, Asian, and Hispanic Clients

Attrition is generally defined as the client's failure to return for therapy. It is estimated that 50% of culturally diverse groups terminate therapy after only one contact with a mental health professional (Boyd-Franklin, 1989; Marin & Marin, 1991; Sue & Sue, 1990; Wilkinson & Spurlock, 1986; Yamamoto, 1986). Several strategies are recommended in the literature to prevent attrition, including telephone calls and letters to remind the client about subsequent therapy sessions, greeting cards sent to the client (e.g., Christmas cards), reduction in the cost of therapy, changes on the schedule for therapy to accommodate the client's own schedule, and so on.

These strategies, however, do not seem to work with culturally diverse groups. An appropriate approach in the prevention of attrition in these groups is probably an emphasis on cultural variables and the impact of these variables on attrition. In general, attention to the series of guidelines described previously across multicultural groups could dramatically reduce attrition among such groups. Tables 7.1, 7.2, 7.3, 7.4, and 7.5 provide a summary of guidelines from prior chapters that are recommended in the prevention of attrition during the process of psychotherapy. These tables

TABLE 7.1 General Guidelines for the Prevention of Attrition

Make sure that the client found what he or she was looking for (e.g., acceptance of the client's belief system).

A quick solution to the problem is expected.

Explore the client's expectation regarding therapy

Involve extended family members in the assessment and treatment process (including biological and nonbiological members). With Asian clients, issues of shame and humiliation may preclude the inclusion of nonbiological members (e.g., friends) in the assessment and treatment of the case.

Explain the reason(s) for reducing the length and frequency of treatment sessions to avoid a perception of lack of interest in working with a given diverse group.

If paraprofessionals are used, do not use them too frequently to prevent the client from feeling that he or she is being treated as a "second-class" client (because he or she is not often seen by professionals).

Use a modality of therapy that is directive, active, and structured, and provide a tentative solution to the core problem (particularly during the first session).

Use mental health professionals (e.g., psychologists, psychiatrists, and social workers) and supporting staff (e.g., secretaries and receptionists) with cross-cultural training.

TABLE 7.2 Guidelines to Prevent Attrition of African American Clients

Discuss racial differences.

Avoid linking mental problems with parents' behaviors; these problems result from environmental conflicts in society.

Do not try to know about family secrets by questioning the client regarding these secrets.

Assure the client(s) that the church can be included in the assessment and treatment of the case.

Do not recommend medication as the first treatment choice; this is an impersonal treatment that may suggest that the therapist does not want to work with the client.

Do not give the impression that you are the "protector of the race" when discussing racial issues.

Referrals made by schools and social welfare agencies may be seen by the client as a threat to his or her autonomy and the possibility of making family secrets public. Discuss this feeling with the client.

TABLE 7.3 Guidelines to Prevent Attrition of Hispanic Clients

Use *formalismo* (formalism) during first contact with the client, but gradually move to *personalismo* (personalism) in subsequent contacts.

Assure the client(s) that the church can be included in the assessment and treatment of the case.

Conduct a brief interview with the father to recognize his authority in the family.

Talk about spiritual events leading to emotional problems (e.g., *mal puesto* [hex] and *mal de ojo* [evil eye]).

Do not provide suggestions that may compete with the belief in *machismo* and *marianismo* (e.g., husband controls the family, and wife is submissive and passive).

During the first session, ensure that client leaves the clinic with concrete recommendations regarding how to handle the problem; avoid the impression that more information is needed in subsequent sessions to provide these recommendations.

Because medication is expected, discuss the possibility of prescribing medication during the first and subsequent sessions.

Time is not a fundamental variable; do not ask client reasons for being late for therapy.

TABLE 7.4 Guidelines to Prevent Attrition of Asian Clients

All Asian clients

   Personalism should be avoided; an emphasis on formalism is expected during the entire process of therapy.

   Disclose educational background to ensure credibility and a sense that the client is with a competent therapist.

   Do not force or encourage the client to reveal his or her problems; wait until the client is ready to discuss these problems. Shame and humiliation suppress the public admission of problems among many Asians.

   Do not recommend the independence of children from their family (particularly their parents).

   Avoid a discussion of hospitalization of the client without considering other alternatives (e.g., home treatment).

Southeast Asian refugees

   Concrete social services should be provided (e.g., housing and school).

   A discussion of traumatic events (e.g., deaths in the family during war) should be considered carefully. A premature discussion of these events could lead to additional stress, which could increase the probability of attrition.

TABLE 7.5 Guidelines to Prevent Attrition of American Indian Clients

---

Emphasize listening rather than talking.

Time is not a fundamental variable; do not ask client reasons for being late for therapy.

Recommend therapies leading to a sense of "working together" to achieve a common goal; competition is not allowed.

Avoid pseudosecrecy statements.

Synthetic medication is not expected, particularly during the first session.

Avoid therapies emphasizing order and authority (e.g., "*I want* you to do . . ." and "*You should* learn how to *control* . . .").

Talk about the "administration" of the problem rather than the "control" of the problem.

Personalism should be avoided.

---

emphasize general guidelines in the prevention of attrition (Table 7.1), followed by specific guidelines recommended for African Americans (Table 7.2), Hispanics (Table 7.3), Asians (Table 7.4), and American Indians (Table 7.5). The generalization of one or more of these guidelines in Tables 7.2, 7.3, 7.4, and 7.5 across groups should be considered in those cases in which the clinician believes that a guideline recommended for a given group may also apply in the case of other multicultural groups.

8

Guidelines for Evaluating and
Using the Epidemiological Mental Health
Literature With Multicultural Groups

A central issue in the assessment and treatment of multicultural groups is the therapist's ability to critically evaluate and use data on the epidemiology of psychiatric disorders or mental problems reported in the literature with these groups. The overall methodology in collecting epidemiological data is to take a sample (e.g., a sample of African Americans, and Hispanics) from a given population (i.e., the population of African Americans, Hispanics, etc.), to screen that sample in relation to the particular variable or event under study (e.g., schizophrenia, depression, phobias), and then to calculate a particular score for that sample. This score is used to estimate the *prevalence* (i.e., the current frequency of that event or variable at the moment the sample was screened) and *incidence* (i.e., number of new cases). Finally, that score (translated into a prevalence or incidence score) is used to make generalizations about the manifestation of that particular variable or event (e.g., the prevalence and incidence of depression) in the particular population from which the sample was originally drawn.

When practitioners read the epidemiological mental health literature involving multicultural groups, the first conclusion they encounter is that the prevalence and incidence of mental disorders is higher among African Americans, Hispanics, Asians, and American Indians in comparison with the white population and other ethnic groups in this country (e.g., Greek, Italian, Irish, and Polish Americans). Among the four target multicultural groups described in this text, the same literature suggests that both the prevalence and incidence of mental disorders are higher in the African American community in comparison with other ethnic groups (Escobar, 1993).

The main guideline for practitioners is to avoid making generalizations from the results published in such literature to the assessment and treatment of culturally diverse groups in their daily clinical practices. In general, three basic reasons support this guideline: (a) a lack of uniformity in the definition of mental problems or psychiatric disorders across epidemiological studies, (b) a lack of cultural validity in most epidemiological studies, and (c) biases in reporting the epidemiology of mental health with culturally diverse groups.

Nonuniformity of Definitions of Mental Disorders

Investigators have not yet agreed on a single instrument to measure the dependent variable (i.e., mental disorder) in psychiatric epidemiology. This means that no uniform definitions of mental disorder exist in studies investigating the prevalence and incidence of these psychiatric disorders (Neighbors & Lumpskin, 1990). For example, Koslow and Rehm (1991) listed 21 instruments that investigators could use to assess the prevalence and incidence of depression in children and adolescents (e.g., Children's Depression Inventory, Children's Depression Scale, the Schedule for Affective Disorders and Schizophrenia for Children, and the Depression Scale Modified for Children). The same problem (i.e., multiple instruments to measure the same mental disorder) is noted in the assessment of depression in adults as well as with respect to other mental disorders (e.g., conduct disorder, attention deficit hyperactivity disorder, schizophrenia, and personality disorders) among both younger and older populations. Thus, epidemiological studies using different instruments in the assessment of prevalence and incidence of such disorders may yield different results across studies in cases in which such instruments do not share the same items, the same number of items, or the same cutoff score (e.g., the score used to determine the presence of depression vs. nondepression).

Thus, when practitioners read that "Black children have been found to exhibit the highest rates of childhood psychopathology and psychiatric impairment" (Ho, 1992, p. 80) or that "prevalence of schizophrenia was found to be highest among African Americans, intermediate among [whites], and lowest among Hispanics" (Escobar, 1993, p. 55) and similar statements involving other culturally diverse groups (Robins & Regier, 1991), it is important to remember that these statements are linked with the results obtained with a particular instrument, and that when a different instrument is used to measure the same event, similar results may not be replicated. It should be recognized that because of the lack of an instrument that could provide a uniform definition of mental disorders across studies, researchers have no choice except to use available instruments that are at least reliable and valid in methodological terms (not necessarily in cultural terms such as in the case of cultural validity discussed later). Researchers, however, are expected to discuss this limitation (i.e., the uniformity of definition of mental disorders) when discussing the applications of their results in clinical practice.

Lack of Cultural Validity

To determine whether the investigator considered the impact of culture in the interpretation of data summarizing the epidemiology of mental health, a practical guideline would be to read the particular study with the following question in mind: Did the study report about the potential effects of language, folk beliefs, and acculturation in the interpretation of the data? If the study did not include sufficient materials to answer this question, the study is probably culturally invalid.

The Effect of Language

Some data suggest that bilingual multicultural clients may be rated with more psychopathology when they are interviewed in English than when they are interviewed in their native language. For example, Marcos, Alpert, Urcuyo, and Kesselman (1973) asked mental health professionals to rate videotapes of either Hispanic clients communicating in Spanish or Hispanic clients communicating in English. Marcos et al. found that more psychopathology was detected by the raters during the English interview. Marcos et al. suggested that when bilingual culturally diverse clients are instructed to speak using English (rather than using their native languages), they may appear tense, uncooperative, and more emotionally withdrawn.

Martinez (1986) pointed out that many Hispanic clients who speak minimal or no English first think in Spanish, then translate from Spanish into English to themselves, and finally respond to the therapist in English during the verbal communicative exchange between the therapist and the client. During this process, many changes in the client's verbal and nonverbal behavior may be interpreted as psychopathological. For example, Hispanic clients with little command of Standard American English would answer a question or remark from the therapist with a simple and restricted verbal output that may be interpreted as a case of "impoverishment of thought." In addition, looking for the right words or sentences in English can create anxiety, leading to "thought derailment" or "loosening of association" (Martinez, 1986, p. 71).

Similar observations have been made about the potential effect of Nonstandard American English versus the effect of Standard American English on the evaluation of psychopathology. For example, Russell (1988) cited a study conducted by D. S. Guy in which white and black therapists observed an actor (playing the role of a client) describing his mental problems in either Black English or Standard American English. Guy found that black therapists reported less psychopathology when the actor spoke in Black English and more psychopathology when the actor spoke in Standard English; the inverse findings were reported by white therapists.

In a similar study, Arroyo (1996) instructed non-Hispanic white psychologists to observe two videotapes. In one videotape, the client had white skin color and spoke Standard English; the second videotape showed the same client with dark skin color and speaking English with a Hispanic accent. In general, raters' inability to empathize with the client, poor prognosis with treatment, and blunted affect were significantly associated with the videotape showing the Hispanic client relative to findings with the non-Hispanic client.

Another important point to consider is whether code switching was allowed during the process of the interview. This phenomenon is defined as "a total or partial language shift with a given situation or conversation" (Russell, 1988, p. 35). Code switching may allow a person to be more or less (depending on the nature of the interview) emotionally distant from important issues in the understanding of the psychiatric problem under consideration (Pitta, Marcos, & Alpert, 1978; Yamamoto, Silva, Justice, Chang, & Leong, 1993). It should be noted that although code switching has been generally associated with bilingual clients in psychotherapy, the same phenomenon is applied in the case of African Americans who, after several minutes during the interviewing process, begin to use Black English, perhaps to provide more information or to become emotionally divorced from the topic under consideration (Russell, 1988).

The following three guidelines are recommended to determine whether a study considered the potential effect of language during the collection of epidemiological data:

1. The interview was conducted either in the interviewee's language (e.g., Spanish), or the potential effect of the second language was considered in the interpretation of the results.

2. The interviewee was allowed to use Nonstandard American English to facilitate both process and content during the interview (e.g., African Americans interviewed in Black English; see Russell, 1988; Yamamoto et al., 1993, p. 113).

3. Code switching was allowed during the process of the interview with bilingual or Nonstandard American English-speaking interviewees.

The Effect of Folk Beliefs

Beliefs in spirits, hexes, and other unseen events are culturally accepted among some members of multicultural groups described in this book. If those beliefs are not considered during the formulation of the clinical diagnosis, the client may be erroneously diagnosed with a psychiatric disorder. For example, if a Hispanic client reports that "An evil eye coming from people I know must be responsible for my bad behavior," a clinician unfamiliar with the place of "evil eye" (*mal de ojo*) in the client's belief system would erroneously conclude that this client is demonstrating a "delusion," which may lead to a diagnosis of schizophrenia (Martinez, 1986). Similarly, if certain items on the Minnesota Multiphasic Personality Inventory (MMPI) such as "Evil spirits possess me at times" are not viewed in the context of clients' beliefs in spirits and hexes (e.g., African Americans and Hispanics), the outcome of the clinical interview would be that the client is mentally ill rather than that the item may represent an assessment of a belief that is culturally accepted by the client and his or her peers sharing the same cultural background (Malgady, Rogler, & Constantino, 1987). Thus, when reading the mental health epidemiological literature, practitioners should look for a description of the potential impact of folk beliefs on results indicating prevalence or incidence of psychiatric disorders among multicultural groups, particularly the Hispanic population.

The Effect of Acculturation

As noted by Dana (1993b, 1995), acculturation is one of the fundamental moderator variables in the interpretation of clinical interview and psychological test data. In the evaluation and interpretation of psychiatric epidemiological data, practitioners are encouraged to screen whether the particular study considered the potential effect of the interpretation of the data. If the study did not include a measure of interpretation and failed to report the potential impact of this variable during the collection of epidemiological data, that study is probably culturally invalid. For example, results obtained with the Developmental Inventory of Black Consciousness and the Racial Identity Attitude Scale, recommended to measure among African Americans, have been related to elevations on the MMPI scales, particularly the F (higher scores suggesting greater psychopathology or deviant response sets), 6 (paranoid), 8 (schizophrenia), and 9 (hypomania) scales (Dana, 1993b). Similarly, Hispanics tend to receive higher MMPI profiles in those cases in which acculturation is not taken into consideration in the interpretation of such profiles (Dana, 1993a, 1995; Montgomery & Orozco, 1985). The same results have been reported with the Rosebud Personal Opinion Survey (Hoffmann, Dana, & Bolton, 1985), which is recommended to measure among American Plains Indians (for a summary of the Plains culture, see Brandon, 1989, pp. 320-349; Force & Force, 1991, pp. 50-53).

An example of lack of cultural validity in a major study in psychiatric epidemiology is the Epidemiologic Catchment Area Study (ECA; Robins & Regier, 1991). In this study, the potential impact of acculturation in the interpretation of the ECA data involving African American and Hispanics (mainly Mexican Americans) was not considered in the major ECA report (Robins & Regier, 1991). In addition, it appears that only the Los Angeles ECA site (among five ECA sites) included a measure of acculturation but only for the Mexican American group (Burnam, Hough, Karno, Escobar, & Telles, 1987). Burnam et al. selected items from the Acculturation Rating Scale for Mexican Americans (Cuellar, Harris, & Jasso, 1980) and the Behavioral Acculturation Scale (Szapocznik, Scopetta, Arnalde, & Kurtines, 1978) and found the following:

> Consistent with the acculturation findings, native-born Mexican Americans, who tended to have high levels of acculturation, had higher lifetime prevalence of disorders (phobias, alcohol abuse or dependence, drug abuse or dependence, as well as major depression and dysthymia) than immigrant Mexican Americans [i.e., the least acculturated group]. (p. 89)

Table 8.1 provides examples of acculturation scales across multicultural groups described in this book that should be included in a given epidemiological study to determine the impact of acculturation on the data collected with these groups.

Biases in Reporting the Epidemiology of Mental Health

The previous discussion emphasizes two issues that may affect the nature of psychiatric epidemiological data: lack of a uniform definition of mental

TABLE 8.1 Acculturation Scales

Scale	Group	Reference
Acculturation Questionnaire	Vietnamese, Nicaraguan refugees	Smither and Rodriguez-Giegling (1982)
Acculturation Rating Scale for Mexican Americans	Mexican Americans	Cuellar, Harris, and Jasso (1980), Cuellar, Arnold, and Maldonado (1995)
Acculturation Balance Scale	Mexican Americans, Japanese	Pierce, Clark, and Kiefer (1972)
Behavioral Acculturation Scale	Cubans	Szapocznik, Scopetta, Arnalde, and Kurtines (1978)
Brief Acculturation Scale for Hispanics	Mexican Americans, Puerto Ricans	Norris, Ford, and Bova (1996)
Children's Acculturation Scale	Mexican Americans	Franco (1983)
Cuban Behavioral Identity Questionnaire	Cubans	Garcia and Lega (1979)
Cultural Life Style Inventory	Mexican Americans	Mendoza (1989)
Developmental Inventory of Black Consciousness	African Americans	Milliones (1980)
Ethnic Identity Questionnaire	Japanese Americans	Masuda, Matsumoto, and Meredith (1970)
Multicultural Acculturation Scale	Southeast Asians, Hispanic Americans, Anglo-Americans	Wong-Rieger and Quintana (1987)
Multicultural Experience Inventory	Mexican Americans	Ramirez (1984)
Racial Identity Attitude Scale	African Americans	Helms (1986)
Rosebud Personal Opinion Survey	American Indians	Hoffman, Dana, and Bolton (1985)
Suinn-Lew Asian Self-Identity Acculturation Scale	Chinese, Japanese, Koreans	Suinn, Rickard-Figueroa, Lew, and Vigil (1987)

disorders and lack of cultural validity. Once the collection of data has been completed, the next step is to translate the data into prevalence and incidence scores. When these scores are reported, however, biases may occur in the actual reporting of the data. The task for practitioners would be to determine in what specific circumstance the reporting of psychiatric epidemiological data involving culturally diverse groups is biased (regardless of the nature of such data). This task may be very difficult to fulfill by practitioners or clinicians who are extremely busy with their clients and have little time for careful reading of the literature. The following three general guidelines will help practitioners to quickly screen biases in reports of epidemiological data collected with culturally diverse groups:

1. Identify the sample (number of African Americans, Hispanics, etc.) from which the data were collected.

2. Determine the population (i.e., how many people in the entire population) from which the sample was selected to reach conclusions regarding the representativeness of the sample (e.g., Is this sample of African Americans representative of the population of African Americans in this country?).

3. Carefully read the conclusions of the study (which summarize major findings in words rather than in complex statistical procedures). If the sample is too small or does not actually represent the particular group under study, the investigator is probably biased in reporting the data. That is, the investigator is assuming that the data can be generalized to the entire population (from which the sample was selected), when, in fact, this may not be true.

The latter guideline may be illustrated using the National Institute of Mental Health Epidemiologic Catchment Area Program, which has been considered "a landmark in psychiatric epidemiology" (Escobar, 1993, p. 51). In this study (Leaf, Meyers, & McEvoy, 1991), 19,182 people, ranging in age from 18 years to 65 years and older, were interviewed in five major U.S. cities between 1978 and 1986 (Baltimore, Durham, New Haven, Los Angeles, and St. Louis). Several important results from this study were summarized by Escobar (1993), including that lifetime prevalences of schizophrenia, manic disorders, and phobias were higher among African Americans than among whites and Hispanics; that the prevalence of alcoholism among younger males was highest among Hispanics and whites and lowest among African Americans, but that among older males (age 45 and older), African Americans had the highest lifetime prevalence rate (i.e., having the symptoms any time during the lifetime of the individual) for alcoholism; and that the lifetime prevalence rate for major depression was higher among whites than among Hispanics and African Americans. In one of the key ECA papers, Robins et al. (1984) concluded that "we might be tempted to infer from these . . . results in the Northeast, mid-Atlantic, and Midwestern areas that *there is* [*sic*] little regional variation in the lifetime prevalence of these disorders *in the United States* [italics added]" (p. 957). In the paper by Keith, Regier, and Rae (1991) summarizing ECA findings on schizophrenic disorders, the authors concluded that they "found a somewhat higher rate of schizophrenia in the U.S. population than rates found in community studies in Europe. . . . We can have considerable confidence in these rates *because of the large sample* [italics added]" (p. 52).

Another example of generalized statements in reporting ECA data is the following: "Lifetime, one-year, and one-month prevalence rates for Hispanic men are higher than for the other two groups [i.e., whites and African Americans]" (Helzer, Burnam, & McEvoy, 1991, p. 86). Similar generalized statements regarding the ECA results can be found in the summary for other psychiatric disorders (Robins & Regier, 1991).

Could the results of the ECA be generalized to the entire population of African Americans and Hispanics in the United States? The answer is probably not. First, lifetime prevalence rates were based on a small number of cases across subsamples. In the ECA study, the number of African Americans across sites ranged from 157 to 1,497, and the total (all sites) was 4,638 (10.4% of the total sample). The number of Hispanics ranged from 17 to 1,458, and the total was 1,600 or 5.5% of the total sample (Leaf et al., 1991, Table 2-5). In 1980 (when most ECA data were collected), the total number of African Americans in the United States between the ages of 15 and 65 years and older was approximately 18.4 million (U.S. Bureau of the Census, 1992), and the total number of Hispanics in the same age range was approximately 15 million. Thus, the ECA study included 0.02% of African Americans and 0.01% of Hispanics from the total number of these culturally diverse groups in 1980. These percentages did not represent the population of African Americans and Hispanics in 1980. Thus, studies reporting prevalence of psychiatric disorders in African Americans and Hispanics using the ECA data set (e.g., Robins et al., 1984) may be considered as biased if such studies fail to mention that readers should consider the results with caution because of the small number of cases in both groups.

In addition, Leaf et al. (1991) reported that a total of 1,600 "Hispanics" were included in the ECA data set. As noted by Escobar (1993), however, the Hispanics in the ECA were largely Mexican Americans. In fact, in the Los Angeles ECA site, 93% of the respondents were Mexican Americans (Escobar, 1993). In this particular case, extrapolations of the ECA conclusions to other Hispanics in the United States (e.g., Cubans, Dominicans, and Puerto Ricans) could also be interpreted as a case of bias in the report of the data (Escobar, 1993). For example, the conclusion that "lifetime . . . prevalence rates [alcoholism] for Hispanic men are higher than for the other two groups" (Helzer et al., 1991, p. 86) would apply only to Mexican Americans.

It should be noted that some ECA investigators have recognized that the ECA results were rarely statistically significant because of the small subsample sizes (e.g., Karno & Golding, 1991, p. 211; Robins et al., 1984, p. 955). In addition, some ECA investigators have also pointed out that a major limitation in that study was that the sample of Hispanics included mainly Mexican Americans and that the other two major Hispanic groups (Cubans and Puerto Ricans) were underrepresented (Leaf et al., 1991). Most studies summarizing the ECA data, however, do not explicitly discuss these limitations.

In the case of the collection of mental health epidemiological data involving American Indians, another example of bias was provided by Thompson, Walker, and Silk-Walker (1993). The data from the Indian Health Service (created in 1955 as part of the U.S. Public Health Service to provide health care for Indians) "are widely quoted as being representative of all Indians" (Thompson et al., 1993, p. 199). A major bias in the reporting of such data, however, is that the Indian Health Service (IHS) only recognizes as "Indians" those living in 32 reservations, which means that Indians from other reservations (approximately 246!) and those living in urban areas are not included in IHS statistics. Thompson et al. also pointed out that "some tribes are *not recognized* by the federal government and, therefore, are not included in most statistics" (p. 199). In this case, if the sample (which only includes those Indians recognized by the federal government) is not representative of the majority of Indians in the continental United States, the obvious conclusion is that a certain degree of bias could be inferred in the report of such data.

In summary, practitioners should read the mental health epidemiological literature with the following guidelines in mind. First, granted that the absence of a uniform definition of mental disorder is an inherent problem in current research, the study should at least use reliable and valid instruments and discuss limitations in the generalization of the data in clinical practice because of that definitional problem. Second, determine the cultural validity of the study (e.g., a discussion regarding the impact of language on the data). Third, determine whether the study included an assessment of acculturation. Fourth, check the population from which the sample was selected and determine whether this sample was representative of that population. Finally, read the conclusions of the study to identify potential biases regarding the generalization of results from the sample to the entire population in language that the reader can understand.

9

Using Culturally
Biased Instruments

Inaccuracies in the assessment and diagnosis of mental disorders can have three consequences: overdiagnosis, underdiagnosis, and misdiagnosis. Biases in testing are generally considered determinant factors in such inaccuracies. Many attempts have been made to eliminate or control biases in the assessment and diagnosis of multicultural groups, including the translation of tests into the language of the group being tested and the development of culturally appropriate norms (Westermeyer, 1993; Yamamoto, 1986). Despite these attempts, the overall sense among researchers and clinicians is that biases in cross-cultural testing are still a reality (Anastasi, 1988; Dana, 1993b). Flaherty et al. (1988) pointed out that culture-free tests (i.e., a test that is not biased against specific culturally diverse groups) must fulfill the following five validity criteria:

1. Content equivalence (Are items relevant for the culture being tested?)
2. Semantic equivalence (Is the meaning of each item the same in each culture?)
3. Technical equivalence (Is the method of assessment comparable across cultures?)
4. Criterion equivalence (Would the interpretation of variables remain the same when compared with the norm for each culture studied?)

5. Conceptual equivalence (Is the test measuring the same theoretical construct across cultures?)

Currently, researchers and clinicians lack a test or assessment of any kind that could fulfill these five validity criteria (Escobar, 1993). This suggests that culture-free tests are not yet available in the assessment of multicultural groups discussed in this book.

Researchers and clinicians, however, agree that despite the reality of bias with most tests or instruments, it is important to use such tests in part because they provide a common language in the assessment and diagnosis of psychiatric disorders by different clinicians (Yamamoto, 1986). In addition, in terms of reimbursement and institutional requirements, many such tests are required in the clinical practice of many therapists involved in the assessment and treatment of mental problems. Therefore, it would be a bad strategy to advise practitioners to stop using these tests or instruments because they are biased (Dana, 1993b). A better strategy is to recognize that it would not be practical (for reasons cited previously) to recommend that practitioners throw out everything that is biased in the process of assessment of multicultural groups (P. Pedersen, personal communication, April 19, 1993) and to determine "how best to utilize [these tests] with patients from a different cultural background" (Yamamoto, 1986, p. 116). The literature suggests at least the following 10 guidelines that practitioners may use to minimize bias during the assessment and diagnosis of multicultural groups using current tests or instruments (Bulhan, 1985; Jenkins & Ramsey, 1991; Wilkinson & Spurlock, 1986):

1. The practitioner should examine his or her own bias and prejudice before engaging in the evaluation of clients who do not share the practitioner's race and ethnicity (see Chapter 1 for a distinction between race and ethnicity concepts).

2. The practitioner should be aware of the potential effect of racism.

3. The practitioner should include an evaluation of socioeconomic variables and use them.

4. The practitioner should try to reduce the sociocultural gap between the client and the person conducting the assessment.

5. The practitioner should include an evaluation of culturally related syndromes.

6. The practitioner should ask culturally appropriate questions.

7. The practitioner should consult paraprofessionals and folk healers within the particular multicultural group.

8. The practitioner should avoid the mental status examination.

9. The practitioner should try to use the least biased assessment strategies first and then consider the most biased strategies in special circumstances.

10. The practitioner should use Dana's (1993a, 1993b) assessment model as an overall approach in minimizing biases.

Examine Biases and Prejudice

Biases in assessment and diagnosis of culturally diverse groups may not necessarily be related to the particular strategy of assessment but rather to bias and prejudices of the practitioner conducting that assessment (Jenkins & Ramsey, 1991). Thus, before using the following guidelines for dealing with biased assessment strategies, it is important for practitioners to make a self-evaluation of the possibility of bias and prejudice in themselves. Jenkins and Ramsey proposed a set of questions dealing with the possibility of bias and prejudice among practitioners interested in working with African American clients. Jenkins and Ramsey suggested that any one of such questions receiving a "not at all" rating (in a very much, somewhat, or not at all format) "means that the therapist is not yet ready to counsel African American [clients] effectively" (Jenkins & Ramsey, 1991, p. 735). As noted by Jenkins and Ramsey, these questions may also be considered with other multicultural groups. Several questions have been added in this text to further assist practitioners in their evaluation of their own bias and prejudice. Table 9.1 provides examples of such questions across culturally diverse groups. Materials in this table could be further modified and extended with the inclusion of additional questions from your own clinical practices with multicultural groups. The rating scale is numbered from 1 (*very much*) to 3 (*not at all*). To determine the overall utility of such questions in a self-assessment of potential bias and prejudice, add all the numbers for all items and divide them by the total number of questions to obtain a bias-prejudice ratio with a given multicultural group. For example, if 1 is checked across all questions dealing with African American clients, the total score will be 10 and the ratio will be 1.0 (or 10/10 = 1.0). This score suggests that the person is probably free of bias and prejudice and ready to conduct assessment and diagnosis with these clients. As the score increases, the potential for bias and prejudice also increases. A score of 3.0 suggests a high level of bias and prejudice; a practitioner receiving this score should either refer the client to another clinician or obtain consultation from other professionals, paraprofessionals, or folk healers within the particular group. A similar assessment of bias and prejudice could be programmed for staff (e.g., other mental health professionals, paraprofessionals, and secretaries). The score obtained from staff could be used to determine whether cross-cultural training is necessary.

Be Aware of the Potential Effects of Racism

When the prevalence and incidence of psychiatric disorders and intelligence test results are explained in terms of differences among races, this explanation is termed *racism*. An emphasis on racism as an "explanation" in this context is considered a fundamental bias because it prevents practitioners from exploring more plausible explanations for the same phenomenon (De La Cancela, 1993).

For example, intelligence test results are generally lower among African Americans, American Indians, Asians, and Hispanics in comparison with scores derived from white subjects (Jenkins & Ramsey, 1991). In the case of African American clients, the diagnosis of schizophrenia is frequently used with these clients in comparison to white clients (Kilkus, Pumariega, & Cuffe, 1995; Wilkinson & Spurlock, 1986). In both cases, the main assumption is that race should play a fundamental role in the explanation of intelligence test results and applications of diagnostic categories involving multicultural groups. When other factors (e.g., social background, income, and educational level) are considered, however, significant differences between whites and culturally diverse groups are not apparent (Escobar, 1993; Jenkins & Ramsey, 1991). If a practitioner makes the mistake of emphasizing racism as an explanation, another negative consequence would be the probability of making an additional error: the overdiagnosing of culturally diverse groups (e.g., "seeing" schizophrenia in an African American client simply because he or she is an African American).

Racism can also lead to underdiagnosis and misdiagnosis. For example, depression has been reported more frequently in white clients compared to African American clients (Wilkinson & Spurlock, 1986). In this case, African American clients who are actually depressed may be underdiagnosed simply because the literature indicates that depression in this group is not as common as depression in the white population or because of the "myth that African Americans could not . . . become depressed" (Griffith & Baker, 1993, p. 161). For example, complaints of headaches, backaches, and pains in the extremities are not considered examples of symptoms for depression in many diagnostic instruments, such as the *Diagnostic and Statistical Manual of Mental Disorders* (*DSM-IV*; American Psychiatric Association, 1994). These

TABLE 9.1 Self-Evaluation of Biases and Prejudices Scale

Question	1 (Very Much)	2 (Somewhat)	3 (Not at All)
1. Have you had formal training with?			
African Americans	1	2	3
American Indians	1	2	3
Asians	1	2	3
Hispanics	1	2	3
Whites	1	2	3
2. Do you have cultural knowledge with?			
African Americans	1	2	3
American Indians	1	2	3
Asians	1	2	3
Hispanics	1	2	3
Whites	1	2	3
3. As parent, would you approve of your son or daughter dating?			
African Americans	1	2	3
American Indians	1	2	3
Asians	1	2	3
Hispanics	1	2	3
Whites	1	2	3
4. Would you date or marry a member from the following group?			
African Americans	1	2	3
American Indians	1	2	3
Asians	1	2	3
Hispanics	1	2	3
Whites	1	2	3
5. Would you feel comfortable providing clinical services to?			
African Americans	1	2	3
American Indians	1	2	3
Asians	1	2	3
Hispanics	1	2	3
Whites	1	2	3
6. Have you been exposed to professional views of?			
African Americans	1	2	3
American Indians	1	2	3
Asians	1	2	3
Hispanics	1	2	3
Whites	1	2	3

TABLE 9.1 *Continued*

Question	1 (Very Much)	2 (Somewhat)	3 (Not at All)
7. Are you familiar with the current literature (journals, books, and periodicals) with?			
African Americans	1	2	3
American Indians	1	2	3
Asians	1	2	3
Hispanics	1	2	3
Whites	1	2	3
8. Would you feel comfortable if you have problems understanding?			
African Americans	1	2	3
American Indians	1	2	3
Asians	1	2	3
Hispanics	1	2	3
Whites	1	2	3
9. Would you expect favorable therapy outcome with?			
African Americans	1	2	3
American Indians	1	2	3
Asians	1	2	3
Hispanics	1	2	3
Whites	1	2	3
10. Would you expect a favorable therapeutic relationship with?			
African Americans	1	2	3
American Indians	1	2	3
Asians	1	2	3
Hispanics	1	2	3
Whites	1	2	3

	Total Score	Ratio[a]
African Americans	_____	_____
American Indians	_____	_____
Asians	_____	_____
Hispanics	_____	_____
Whites	_____	_____

a. For example, if 1 is circled for all questions involving African Americans, the total score is 10 and the ratio is 1.0 (or 10 ÷ 10). The maximum bias-prejudice ratio is 3.0, suggesting a high degree of bias and prejudice toward a given group.

symptoms, however, may suggest depression in an African American client (Wilkinson & Spurlock, 1986, p. 23).

Similarly, depression among Asians may be underdiagnosed because of the tendency of this group to display only somatic symptoms of depression (e.g., weight loss) and not because of their race per se (Yamamoto, Silva, Justice, Chang, & Leong, 1993). Asians also tend to show lower prevalence and incidence of psychiatric disorders in the epidemiological literature (Jenkins & Ramsey, 1993), and this finding is probably related to the cultural value of "shame" that prevents Asians from making public their problems (Sue & Sue, 1990). In this finding, the Asian status may be irrelevant.

Autism is rarely diagnosed among African American children in comparison with white children. Wilkinson and Spurlock (1986) suggest that "there is a strong probability that instead of [autism] being rare, it frequently may be diagnosed erroneously as mental retardation" (p. 22). If true, this is an example of misdiagnosis.

Race seems to play a major role in the manifestation of mental disorders in the previous examples. If the client is white, mental problems A, B, and C are expected (according to mental health epidemiological data). Similarly, if the patient is an African American, mental problems D, E, and F are expected. This conclusion, however, may "reflect biases in the assignment of diagnosis according to race" (Wilkinson & Spurlock, 1986, p. 17).

Include and Use an Evaluation
of Socioeconomic Variables

During the first session with African American, Hispanic, Asian, and American Indian clients, practitioners often collect social and economic data (e.g., income level, urban vs. rural locations, parents' education, prenatal care, parenting, and contacts with welfare agencies). During the clinical assessment of the case and the assignment of the particular diagnosis, however, socioeconomic variables are rarely considered. Mental health problems, however, frequently are more prevalent and have a higher incidence in lower socioeconomic families (Jenkins & Ramsey, 1991; Wilkinson & Spurlock, 1986, p. 22; Yamamoto, 1986, p. 108). Many members of multicultural groups discussed in this book are from low socioeconomic families. An assessment of these groups without taking into consideration the impact of socioeconomic variables could lead to bias in the assignment of diagnoses.

For example, studies assessing the mental health status of Vietnamese refugees revealed that symptoms of depression were noted when the head of the family did not have a job (Yamamoto, 1986, p. 108). This observation has also been confirmed with other multicultural groups. For example, in the Hispanic Health and Nutrition Examination study (Escobar, 1993), Puerto Ricans were not only the most socioeconomically disadvantaged among the Hispanics (in comparison with Mexican Americans and Cubans) but also had a significantly higher prevalence of major depressive disorders.

Minimize the Sociocultural Gap

Some findings suggest that inaccuracies in the assessment and diagnosis of mental disorders may be the result of a difference between the therapist's and the client's sociocultural background (Jackson, Berkowitz, & Farley, 1974). In these findings, the greater the difference in sociocultural variables, the less accurate the assessment and diagnosis.

For example, African Americans often obtain lower scores on intelligence tests when such tests are administered by white practitioners rather than by African American clinicians (Jenkins & Ramsey, 1991). Other studies have shown that African Americans tend to alter their responses on self-report measures when the race of the examiner changes (Lineberger & Calhound, 1983). In addition, Marcos (1976) and Marcos, Alpert, Urcuyo, & Kesselman (1973) suggested that when bilingual Hispanic clients are interviewed in English rather than in their native language (i.e., Spanish) the probability of errors in assessment and diagnosing of psychiatric disorders may increase. Thus, to minimize biases in the assessment and diagnosis of culturally diverse groups using standard instruments, effort should be directed to minimize the sociocultural gap between the examiner and the client.

Sue (1988) suggested that ethnic match seems more important than racial match in minimizing biases. This suggestion implies, for example, that if the examiner and the client do not share the same race (e.g., white examiners working with highly acculturated Hispanic clients) but share similar values and lifestyles, potential biases in the assessment and diagnosis of that client may be minimized. In this example, ethnic match (e.g., sharing similar values) seems more relevant than racial match (i.e., examiners and clients from the same racial group) in preventing bias. Sue (1988) also suggests that if examiners and clients are from the same racial group (e.g., Asian examiners and Asian clients) but do not share similar cultural values (e.g., acculturated Asian examiners vs. recent Asian immigrants), biases in the assessment and diagnosis of such clients may increase. In this example, racial match seems less important than cultural match (Sue, 1988). Thus, in the current guideline, an emphasis on ethnic match between examiners and clients is suggested to minimize bias in the assessment process.

Include an Evaluation of
Cultural-Related Syndromes

In the literature, culture-specific disorders are known as "cultural-bound syndromes." Because many of these syndromes have been noted across different cultures, Simons and Hughes (1993) proposed the term cultural-related syndromes.

Examples of cultural-related syndromes that practitioners are most likely to find in their practices include the following (Griffith & Baker, 1993; Rubel, O'Nell, & Collado-Ardon, 1984; Simons & Hughes, 1993):

- *Ataque de nervios* among Hispanics (i.e., out-of-consciousness state resulting from evil spirits)
- *Amok* and *mal de pelea* among clients from Malaysia, Laos, Philippines, Polynesia, Papua New Guinea, and Puerto Rico (a dissociative disorder involving outbursts of violent and aggressive or homicidal behavior directed at people and objects)
- *Dhat* in the Indian, Chinese, and Sri Lankan communities (extreme anxiety associated with a sense of weakness, exhaustion, and the discharge of semen)
- Falling-out in African American communities (seizure-like symptoms resulting from traumatic events such as robberies)
- Ghost sickness among American Indians (weakness and dizziness resulting from the action of witches and evil forces)
- *Hwa-byung* in the Asian communities (pain in the upper abdomen, fear of death, and tiredness resulting from the imbalance between reality and anger)
- *Koro* among the Asians (a man's desire to grasp his penis resulting from the fear that it will retract into his body and cause death)
- *Pibloktog* in the case of clients from the Arctic and subarctic Eskimo communities (excitement, coma, and convulsive seizures resembling an abrupt dissociative episode, often associated with amnesia, withdrawal, irritability, and irrational behaviors such as breaking furniture, eating feces, and verbalization of obscenities)
- *Taijin kyofusho* in the case of Asians (guilt about embarrassing others and timidity resulting from the feeling that the appearance, odor, or facial expressions are offensive to other people)
- *Mal puesto,* hex, root-work, and voodoo death among African American and Hispanics (unnatural diseases and death resulting from the power of people who use evil spirits)
- *Susto, espanto, pasmo,* and *miedo* in the case of Hispanics (tiredness and weakness resulting from frightening and startling experiences)

- *Wacinko,* an American Indian's feeling of anger, withdrawal, mutism, or suicide resulting from reaction to disappointment and interpersonal problems
- Wind and cold illness in the case of Hispanics and Asians (a fear of the cold and the wind; feeling weakness and susceptibility to illness resulting from the belief that natural and supernatural elements are not balanced)

Assuming that clinicians agree that it is important to consider the impact of cultural-related syndromes on the assessment of multicultural groups discussed in this book, a crucial question would be, Why are such syndromes not considered by clinicians in their clinical practices? At least two answers are proposed.

First, current standard clinical ratings and diagnostic instruments do not include criteria for the assessment of such syndromes. For example, clinical ratings, such as the MMPI, the Child Behavior Checklist, and the Zung Depression Scale, as well as diagnostic instruments, such as the *DSM-IV* and the Schedule of Affective Disorders and Schizophrenia (Rutter, Tuma, & Lann, 1988), do not require or do not include or both an assessment of such syndromes to distinguish between these syndromes and "true" psychopathology. Thus, clinicians may not be concerned about the screening of cultural-related syndromes when making a diagnosis of mental disorders with a given client from any of the multicultural groups discussed in this book. In the case of the *DSM-IV,* an outline of cultural formulation and a summary of major culturally bound syndromes are included in response to recommendations from experts to consider the impact of cultural variables in the diagnosis of psychiatric disorders (Cervantes & Arroyo, 1994; Rogler, 1993). Practitioners using the *DSM-IV,* however, are not required to consider the presence of these variables in their *DSM-IV* multiaxial evaluation. Practitioners are simply encouraged to consider these variables when making a psychiatric diagnosis; they are not required to explicitly deal with these variables when recording the results of a *DSM-IV* multiaxial evaluation. As noted in Chapter 10, however, a major contribution in the *DSM-IV* is the inclusion of "specific culture" features in the description of several psychiatric disorders and a summary of culturally bound syndromes.

Second, reimbursement for clinical practices regarding cultural-related syndromes is not a practice among major private insurance, Medicaid, and Medicare. For example, a practitioner cannot expect to receive payment for the assessment and treatment of cultural-related syndromes such as susto, ghost sickness, mal puesto, koro, or ataque de nervios. A clinician in private practice would not be expected to spend time screening such syndromes in those cases in which his or her efforts will not lead to reimbursement.

A distinction should be made between considering the assessment of such syndromes only in those cases in which reimbursement for clinical assessment of such syndromes is available and the assessment of these syndromes because it is, indeed, important to ensure that a culturally diverse client is having a mental problem rather than a manifestation of cultural-related syndromes. The first point is a matter of money; the second is a matter of ethical standards leading to a recognition of cultural competence in the practice of a clinician involved in the assessment of multicultural groups discussed in this book. An important guideline to prevent unfair discriminatory practices and unethical behaviors in the assessment of African American, American Indian, Asian, and Hispanic clients is to have some familiarity with cultural-related syndromes shared by members of the particular groups. In addition, the clinician should formulate a list of symptoms suggesting the presence of these cultural-related syndromes for consideration before a psychiatric diagnosis is applied to the particular client (American Psychological Association, 1992). Consultations with family members and peers within the particular groups should also be considered.

For example, if an American Indian client reports that "I believe that my weakness, loss of appetite, fainting are the result of the action of witches and evil supernatural forces," this statement would be an example of schizophrenia to a clinician unfamiliar with the effect of ghost sickness among American Indians. If this belief is not shared by family members or peers, it is probably not a culturally supported belief (Westermeyer, 1993) within that particular group. Because current clinical ratings and diagnostic instruments do not include criteria for the assessment of such syndromes in clinical practices, to apply these guidelines, practitioners would have to develop their own system of assessment of cultural-related syndromes.

Despite the importance of considering these cultural-related syndromes in clinical practices, too much emphasis on cultural-related syndromes may prevent practitioners from considering that many of these syndromes may actually include symptoms of severe psychiatric disorders. This emphasis could not only lead to misdiagnosis of real psychiatric disorders but also result in turning clients over to folk healers for treatment under the assumption that what the client has is a cultural-related syndrome that cannot be treated by mental health professionals. As noted by Westermeyer (1993), turning multicultural clients over to folk healers because the presenting symptoms are examples of a cultural-related condition may lead to a major error in clinical practices. Thus, it is advisable to assume that all cultural-related syndromes are potential cases of severe psychiatric disorders until further cross-cultural assessment reveals that culture is the major element in the manifestation of such syndromes. The assumption here is that if culture is the major element, the client does not require psychiatric treatment.

Ask Culturally Appropriate Questions

During the interviewing process, a culturally appropriate line of questioning should be used to avoid misunderstanding and errors in the diagnosis of culturally diverse groups. This guideline will be illustrated with examples involving Asian clients. Similar examples might be generalized to other multicultural groups.

The questions, "What is your opinion of yourself compared with other people?" and "Do you feel better, or not as good, or about the same as most?" are not always appropriate with Asian clients (Yamamoto, 1986, p. 112). Asians, in general, do not like to compare themselves with other people. An Asian client may not answer the question, "Are you angry with your parents?" because he or she always shows respect toward parents (particularly the elderly), even if the relationship between a son or daughter and parents is not good. A practitioner unfamiliar with these cultural values would mistakenly use such values in the diagnosis of the client. In the first example, more appropriate questions would be "Do you like yourself?" or "Do you feel okay about yourself as a person?" (Yamamoto, 1986, p. 112). In the second example, Gaw (1993) suggested the question, "How is the relationship between you and your [parents]?" (p. 274).

Consult Paraprofessionals and Folk Healers
Within a Multicultural Group

Bias in the process of assessment and diagnosis with culturally diverse groups could be minimized if the clinician is assisted (in that process) by people within the particular group. The ideal strategy will be to include mental health professionals within the multicultural group. This strategy, however, is difficult to implement because of the shortage of African American (1.2%), American Indian (0.2%), Asian (1.0%), and Hispanic (0.7%) mental health professionals (Russo, Olmedo, Stapp, & Fulcher, 1981). A practical, and more realistic, strategy is to use paraprofessionals and folk healers within the particular multicultural group.

For example, Southeast Asian refugees sometimes feel insecure and threatened in unfamiliar settings (e.g., the office of a white therapist), which may lead to suspiciousness or mistrust resembling "paranoid symptoms" (Westermeyer, 1993). A paraprofessional Southeast Asian refugee, however, will quickly indicate that these "symptoms" are expected in refugees who experienced repressive regimes and survived concentration camps.

In the case of African American and Hispanic clients, consultation with the *espiritista, curandero,* or folk healer is recommended in those cases in which African American and Hispanic clients are evaluated with the MMPI and happen to check "true" on items such as "Evil spirits possess me at times," "I believe I am being plotted against," "I believe I am a condemned person," and so on. According to the profiles of the MMPI, these items are examples of individuals who exhibit paranoid or schizophrenic symptoms. These items, however, may be endorsed by African Americans and Hispanics, for example, who generally believe in evil spirits, the action of witches, and malevolent supernatural powers (Martinez, 1986). Because of the central role of the medicine man or woman among American Indian clients, these healers should always be consulted before reaching conclusions regarding the diagnosis and treatment of these clients (Walker & LaDue, 1986, pp. 176-177).

Avoid the Mental Status Examination

Clinicians often use the mental status exam to reinforce clinical data obtained with standard clinical rating and diagnostic instruments. This exam makes the assumption that a series of "normal" behaviors and cognitive processes are shared by normal people, regardless of cultural background. This assumption, however, could dramatically multiply the impact of existing bias in current clinical ratings and diagnostic instruments (Hughes, 1993). The following examples of components of the mental status examination and their potential bias when used with multicultural groups may explain why the current guideline suggests that it may be appropriate to avoid the mental status examination with multicultural groups discussed in this book (Hughes, 1993; Mueller, Kiernan, & Langston, 1992; Westermeyer, 1993).

During the assessment of concentration and vigilance, clients receive the serial 7s test, in which the client is asked to subtract 7 from 100 and then to continue subtracting 7 from each answer. If the client has a problem in mastering this task, an assumption of anxiety, depression, and schizophrenia is formulated. If this assumption is "confirmed" with scores derived from a clinical rating scale, the practitioner would think that he or she is on the "right track." Aside from the fact that the validity of this test is questioned by many researchers (see Hughes, 1993, pp. 27-28), many members of multicultural groups would fail this task because they are not versed in the area of counting forward or backward.

The assessment of orientation allows clinicians to assess negativism, confusion, distraction, hearing impairment, and receptive language disorders. This test emphasizes the assessment of the self (the person), place, and time. For example, a therapist would ask, "What is your last name?" "What is the name of this month?" and "Where are you right now?" In response to the first question, a Hispanic client may look confused and distracted because he or she would have to decide which last name of the two last names to report (Hispanics often have one last name for the father [e.g., Rodriguez] and another for the mother [e.g., Arias], such as Federico Antonio Rodriguez Arias). If the client is not familiar with the name of the month in Standard American English or is not familiar with the name of the building (or cannot remember the name), and he or she appears to provide incorrect answers, the practitioner would assume that the client is exhibiting negativism, hearing impairment, or receptive language disorder.

The assessment of general knowledge could be used to assess poor educational background, severe deterioration in intellectual functioning, and the ability to assess remote memory. For example, a clinician could ask, "What are the colors of the American flag?" "How far is it from Houston to Chicago?" "What are the names of three countries in Central America?" "Who is the president of the United States?" "Who was the president before him?" and "What is the total population of the United States of America?" As noted by Hughes (1993), the answers to such questions imply geographical and public knowledge; many members of multicultural groups do not have this kind of knowledge for two reasons: They are too poor to travel (which is one way to answer some of these questions), and many members in such groups are illiterate (Westermeyer, 1993). In addition, clients with different cultural backgrounds would perform poorly on this test.

The assessment of the thought process is a crucial area. For example, thought blocking is a sudden cessation of thought or speech that suggests schizophrenia, depression, and anxiety (Mueller et al., 1992). Clients who are not fluent in English might show thought blocking. Clients with little command of Standard American English would spend a great deal of time looking for the correct word, phrase, or sentence before answering a question; this could create anxiety resulting in thought blocking (Martinez, 1986). African Americans who use black English in most conversational contexts would also spend a great deal of time attempting to construct phrases or sentences in Standard American English when they feel that Standard American English is expected in certain circumstances (Dillard, 1973; Yamamoto et al., 1993).

Appearance is another important element in the mental status examination. For example, lack of eye contact, failure to stare directly into the therapist's eyes, and careless or bizarre dress and grooming could point to signs of psychiatric disorders (Hughes, 1993). Many clients from the multicultural groups described in this book avoid eye contact and staring at people's eyes during social interactions (Hughes, 1993; Sue & Sue, 1990), partially because in such groups it is impolite to maintain eye contact or to look directly into the eyes of other persons. The therapist's definition of what is normal dress and grooming is not shared by a client who visits the therapist after finishing a long working day as a garage mechanic. This client will probably look dirty, with a soiled face, hands, and nails and a careless appearance.

To appreciate why multicultural groups discussed in this book may have difficulties with the components of the mental status examination and why such difficulties could increase bias in the assessment of these groups, try to picture yourself in the place of one of these groups and attempt to deal with the elements of that exam. Would you pass these tests? For example, subtract 7 from 100 and continue doing this until you get the lower number (can you mention this number as you read this line?). Prior studies suggest that normal subjects can make between 3 and 12 errors with this test (Hughes, 1993). Now, try the orientation test; could you name the location and the building you are placed in after you have experienced a panic attack in an unfamiliar city? In the case of the general knowledge test, can you name the capital of three countries in the Middle East, the distance from New York to Los Angeles, the distance from the sun to the earth, the distance from your house to your parents' house, the colors in your state flag, and the main difference between the U.S. flag and the Malaysian flag? For the assessment of your thought process, pretend that you are not fluent in Spanish and visit Mexico City; would you take time to think about what you want to say before you open your mouth and say it? Will you look up and down, looking for the right phrase, word, or sentence before you order lunch? To determine what people may think about the way you dress, pretend that you are a Puerto Rican taxi driver in New York City, and at 3:00 p.m. on a hot summer day, you realize that you have your first appointment with the therapist and decide to keep your appointment; later, you learned that the therapist made a note that you were probably depressed or psychotic because you dressed carelessly and had dirty nails and hands and a soiled face. Knowing that you did not have time to go home to take a shower, shave, and change clothes, would you return for a second appointment?

Try to Use the Least Biased
Assessment Strategies First

A review of the literature suggests that there is an order concerning the degree of bias across assessment strategies (e.g., Dana, 1993b; Jenkins &

Ramsey, 1991). In summarizing that degree of bias across strategies, the order (from less to more bias as the number increases) is as follows:

1. Physiological assessment (e.g., the use of electrodermal activity in the assessment of psychopathology; Boucsein, 1992)
2. Direct behavioral observations (e.g., the percentage of intervals during which African American and white children display attention to task materials; Anderson, 1988; Paniagua & Black, 1990)
3. Self-monitoring (e.g., clients record their own overt or covert behaviors, such as obsessive thoughts and number of tasks completed, respectively)
4. Behavioral self-report rating scales (e.g., Fear Survey Schedule; Wolpe & Lang, 1964)
5. Clinical interview (which includes the mental status examination)
6. Trait measures (e.g., California Psychological Inventory; Dana, 1993b)
7. Self-report of psychopathology measures (e.g., MMPI and Beck Depression Inventory; Dana, 1993a, 1995)
8. Projective tests with structured stimuli (e.g., Tell-Me-a-Story Test; Constantino, Malgady, & Rogler, 1988; Malgady, Constantino, & Rogler, 1984)
9. Projective tests with ambiguous stimuli (e.g., Rorschach test; Dana, 1993b)

All assessment strategies listed previously have some degree of bias (Dana, 1993a; Jenkins & Ramsey, 1991). The important guideline to remember, however, is to emphasize assessment strategies in which interpretations and speculations are minimized. For example, the level of interpretations and speculations is much greater with projective tests compared to direct behavioral observations. Thus, in comparison with projective tests, bias might be greatly reduced when direct behavioral observations (or behavioral assessment strategies) are programmed to measure the particular event (e.g., number of times a depressed client refuses to eat or does not participate in social activities).

Some practitioners use only behavioral assessment in the evaluation of their clients (e.g., behavior analysts). The majority of practitioners, however, use a combination of trait measures, intelligence measures, self-report of psychopathology measures, and projective measures. If these measures are used, the practitioner should make an effort to select those measures with evidence of cross-cultural validity. Table 9.2 includes examples of tests recommended with culturally diverse groups. Tests in Table 9.2 may minimize bias, but total elimination of biases is not expected (Dana, 1993b; French, 1993; Lopez & Nunez, 1987). A review of these tests can be found in Dana (1993b).

TABLE 9.2 Tests Recommended for Culturally Diverse Groups

Name	Area	Reference
Center for Epidemiologic Studies Depression Scale (CES-D)	Depression	Radloff (1977)
Culture Fair Intelligence Test	Intelligence	Anastasi (1988)
Draw-a-Person Test (DAP)	Projective	French (1993)
Eysenck Personality Questionnaire (EPQ)	Personality	Eysenck and Eysenck (1975)
Holtzman Inkblot Technique (HIT)	Projective	Holtzman (1988)
Kaufman Assessment Battery for Children (K-ABC)	Intelligence	Kaufman, Kamphaus, and Kaufman (1985)
Leiter International Performance Scale	Intelligence	Anastasi (1988)
Progressive Matrices	Intelligence	Anastasi (1988)
Schedule for Affective Disorders and Schizophrenia (SADS)	Most disorders	Spitzer and Endicott (1978)
System of Multicultural Pluralistic Assessment (SOMPA)	Intelligence	Mercer and Lewis (1978)
Tell-Me-a-Story Test (TEMAS)	Personality and cognition	Constantino, Malgady, and Rogler (1988)

Use Dana's Assessment Model

Dana (1993a, 1993b) provides an assessment model that clinicians may use in combination with the previous guidelines in an overall approach to minimizing biases during the assessment of multicultural groups. Dana recommends five steps in the application of his model.

Conduct an Assessment of Acculturation

Dana (1993a) emphasizes that this assessment "should be administered and interpreted prior to application of any assessment procedures whatsoever" (p. 10). Chapter 8 includes examples of acculturation scales across multicultural groups discussed in this text.

Provide a Culture-Specific Service Delivery Style

This step emphasizes the provision of "behavioral etiquettes" that facilitate a task-oriented approach and a trusting client-therapist relationship necessary to initiate and complete the testing procedures. For example, with Hispanic clients, the use of Señor (Mr.), Señora (Mrs.), or Señorita (Miss) in an environment including features (e.g., pictures and furniture) from that particular racial or ethnic group could greatly enhance the testing process.

Use the Client's Native Language (or Preferred Language)

For example, Hispanic and Asian American clients may be told, "Perhaps you would feel more comfortable if we do this test in your native language. If you prefer to do this test in English, please let me know about your preference."

Select Assessment Measures Appropriate for the Cultural Orientation and Client Preferences

Dana (1993a, 1993b) recommends the use of culture-specific instruments and an assessment process tailored for less acculturated clients. This guideline represents the emic perspective in the assessment of multicultural groups, which emphasizes an understanding of clients in their cultural context. For example, behavioral observation (either in the clinic or at home) would be recommended to understand how Hispanic families interact verbally and nonverbally. The use of life history reports may provide Asian, Hispanic, or American Indian clients with the opportunity to talk about their problems using culture-specific modes of communication (e.g., language and gestures). The tests listed in Table 9.2 are also recommended (see also Dana, 1993b, pp. 141-167).

Use a Culture-Specific Strategy When Informing the Client About Findings Derived From the Assessment Process

The applicability of this step can be illustrated with examples from the MMPI scales (Graham, 1990) and subscales from the Wechsler Adult Intelligence Scale (WAIS; e.g., Golden, 1990). (The same culture-specific strategy is recommended when reporting findings derived from other measures.) Parents of a Hispanic adolescent client could be told, "I understand that in the Hispanic culture, many people believe that they can be affected by evil spirits. Perhaps the finding with this test [e.g., MMPI] suggests that your son is expressing this cultural belief rather than being really crazy" (meaning "loco," which implies a more severe condition in the mind of many Hispanics). Similarly, an American Indian client may be told,

> This finding suggests that you have low self-esteem, are reserved and timid, lack interest in activities, and that you are a shy person. My understanding, however, is that among American Indians, these behaviors are culturally accepted in their tribes. So, we probably need to talk more about these behaviors to ensure that they are not part of the clinical diagnosis of the mental problem you reported earlier to me.

The K scale is one of the validity scales used to detect instances of test bias during the interpretation of results derived from the clinical scales of the MMPI profiles. An extremely low score on the K scale suggests, among other things, that the client is skeptical and tends to be suspicious about the motivations of other people. Cultural paranoia could explain why an African American client has a low score on the K scale. In the case of Asian clients, the expression of psychological problems in terms of somatic complaints is a culturally accepted phenomenon. For this reason, with Asian clients, an elevation on the Hypochondriasis Scale should be interpreted in terms of this cultural phenomenon.

I. Cuellar (personal communication, January 1994) suggests that the client may not admit that he or she is actually suffering a mental problem if given the option (e.g., in the presence of the MMPI scores) to interpret the problem in terms of cultural variables. Cuellar suggests that an alternative approach would be to sit down with the client or family members or both and discuss possible cultural explanations. On the basis of this informal discussion, the clinician could then decide if cultural variables explain test findings. In this case, the opinion of the client or family members or both regarding the interpretation of test data in terms of cultural variables is minimal.

In the case of the WAIS (and the same test for children), Golden (1990) pointed out that this test "remains heavily influenced by cultural and language concepts that reflect the life of the average American, but not that of most [multicultural] groups" (p. 46). This observation is particularly true for the performance by members of these groups on the Information, Comprehension, Vocabulary, Picture Completion, and Picture Arrangement subtests that are associated with alternate cultural background. For example, a Hispanic client may receive a very low score on the Information subtest (e.g., below 5, where a mean is 10 and the standard deviation is 3) not because the client is not intelligent but because he or she lacks information regarding the total population, height of women, number of senators, and other "general knowledge" expected from the average American in the United States. A similar point could be made in the interpretation of the scores with the Comprehension (the client may not be able to understand basic U.S. customs and situations), Vocabulary (the client cannot define a word using Standard American English), Picture Completion (the client cannot complete the picture because he or she is not familiar with the objects pictured in the American culture), and Picture Arrangement (the client cannot arrange the pictures to tell a logical and coherent story because the social sequence required on the test is not part of the client's cultural background) subtests.

In each example, the task for the therapist engaged in the assessment of these groups (particularly Hispanics and Asians) will be to explain to his or her clients the potential impact of cultural variables on these scores. For example, in the case of the Vocabulary subtest, the therapist could say to a Hispanic client, "Your score on this test is very low. Perhaps you have problems communicating in English. I will repeat the same test using words from your own language" (translations of the WAIS are available in Spanish and other languages).

As noted by Golden (1990) and Sue and Sue (1990), many mental health professionals (particularly within the African American and Hispanic communities) have suggested that all Wechsler tests (and other individual intelligence tests, such as the Stanford-Binet) are biased against multicultural groups (particularly African Americans and Hispanics). As noted at the beginning of this chapter, however, suggesting the exclusion of these tests from the practices of many clinicians is a bad tactic. Teaching practitioners how to interpret biased tests (e.g., the WAIS) using cross-cultural skills seems more appropriate. For example, in the previous case involving the score on the Information subtest, a low score could be used to suggest brain damage (Golden, 1990); however, a clinician with cross-cultural skills in this area would quickly point out that the client scored low on that subtest probably because he or she did not have the information expected of people familiar with the American culture.

10

Using Cultural Variables in the
*Diagnostic and Statistical Manual
of Mental Disorders*

A major contribution in the *Diagnostic and Statistical Manual of Mental Disorders* (*DSM-IV*; American Psychiatric Association, 1994) is an emphasis on the need to consider the potential impact of cultural variables in the assessment and diagnosis of psychiatric disorders. Practitioners unfamiliar with the impact of these variables on assessment and diagnosis of psychiatric disorders "may incorrectly judge as psychopathology those normal variations in behavior, belief, or experience that are particular to the individual's culture" (*DSM-IV*, 1994, p. xxiv).

Practitioners are not required to include these variables in the *DSM-IV* (1994) multiaxial classification. This would require a new axis specifically dealing with cultural-bound syndromes and cultural criteria associated with these syndromes. As noted earlier, if these syndromes are used to diagnose a client, the clinician will not be reimbursed by insurance companies, Medicaid, and Medicare because these entities do not have a provision for covering such syndromes.

Despite this limitation, practitioners concerned with the underrepresentation of cultural considerations in the assessment and diagnosis of multicultural groups will agree that the *DSM-IV* (1994) has made a tremendous contribution in terms of encouraging clinicians to seriously consider cultural variables when making a diagnosis of mental disorders among clients from the four multicultural groups described in this book (Moffic & Kinzie, 1996).

The *DSM-IV* (1994) includes three recommendations for dealing with cultural and ethnic variations in the assessment and diagnosis of psychiatric disorders. Two recommendations are included in Appendix I: A summary of culture-bound syndromes and guidelines regarding cultural formulations that clinicians should consider to explore the impact of the client's culture on diagnosis. The third recommendation is a "discussion . . . of cultural variations in the clinical presentations of those disorders . . . included in the DSM-IV Classification" (p. xxiv). These cultural variations, however, were not described across the entire *DSM-IV* classification of mental disorders. In addition, whereas some disorders include a discussion of these variations with specific examples provided by the *DSM-IV,* other disorders include only these variations without examples. Busy clinicians may not have time to carefully screen this recommendation across the *DSM-IV.* This chapter will assist practitioners with a quick screening of psychiatric disorders involving this recommendation and examples provided in the *DSM-IV* (Table 10.1), with a summary of disorders with these recommendations but without examples (Table 10.2), and a summary of disorders with neither discussion of cultural variations nor examples (Table 10.3). This chapter will also discuss the potential impact of cultural variations in the case of some of the "Other Conditions That May Be a Focus of Clinical Attention" (pp. 675-686).

Several points should be noted to understand the logistics in the construction of Tables 10.1, 10.2, and 10.3. Cultural variations in the *DSM-IV* (1994) are sometimes recommended (under the heading "Specific Culture, Age, and Gender Features") for the overall set of disorders (e.g., mental retardation) but not for the subtypes within the set (e.g., mild, moderate, severe, and profound mental retardation). For example, *DSM-IV* recommended that "care should be taken to ensure that intellectual testing procedures reflect adequate attention to the individual's ethnic or cultural background" (p. 44). *DSM-IV* suggested that this general cultural variation should be used during the diagnosis of all subtypes of mental retardation.

In other instances, *DSM-IV* (1994) recommended a general statement regarding cultural variations for a set of disorders (e.g., mood disorders and personality disorders), but only some subtypes during the set received these variations. For example, *DSM-IV* provided a description of cultural variations for all mood disorders. In the case of depressive disorders, however, only major depressive disorders received a description of such variations (Table 10.1); specific cultural variations were not given for dysthymic

TABLE 10.1 *DSM-IV* (1994) Disorders With Cultural Variations and Examples

Disorder	*Subtype*
Attention deficit and disruptive behavior disorders	*Conduct disorder*
	May be misapplied to individuals residing in settings (e.g., threatening, high-crime, and impoverished areas) in which undesirable behaviors could be considered protective. Immigrant youth from countries with a history of aggressive behaviors (necessary for their survival in such countries) resulting from a long history of wars would not warrant the diagnosis of conduct disorder. If the behavior is the result of the reaction to the immediate social context, it would not be diagnosed as conduct disorder.
Delirium and dementia	*All subtypes*
	Clients from certain cultures may be unfamiliar with the information included in tests used to measure general knowledge, memory, and orientation.
Alcohol-related disorders	*All subtypes*
	Alcohol use patterns could be the result of cultural traditions in which the consumption of alcohol is expected in family, religious, and social settings, particularly during childhood. Among Asians, the prevalence of alcohol consumption is generally lower than that of other countries. Low educational level, unemployment, and lower socioeconomic status are often associated with alcohol consumption. In the United States, the prevalence of alcohol-related disorders is often higher among Hispanic males than among white and African American males.
Caffeine-related disorders	*All subtypes*
	Caffeine use varies widely across cultures. For example, in most developing countries, caffeine use is less than 50 mg/day in comparison with 400 mg/day or more in Sweden, the United States, and some European countries.
Schizophrenia and other psychotic disorders	*All subtypes*
	If clinicians and clients do not share the same race and ethnicity, cultural differences between them should be considered. Delusional ideas (e.g., witchcraft) and auditory hallucinations (e.g., seeing the Virgin Mary or hearing God's voice) may be abnormal in one culture and normal in other cultures. Variability in language, style of emotional expressions, body language, and eye contact across cultures should be considered when assessing symptoms of schizophrenia. Catatonic behavior is more common in non-Western countries.

TABLE 10.1 *Continued*

Disorder	Subtype
Schizophrenia and other psychotic disorders (continued)	*Schizophreniform disorder*
	In addition to the previous cultural variations and examples, in developing countries, recovery from psychotic disorders is often more rapid, which may result in higher rates of schizophreniform disorder than of schizophrenia.
	Schizoaffective disorder
	The same cultural variations and examples as described for schizophrenia apply for this disorder.
	Brief psychotic disorder
	This disorder should be distinguished from culturally sanctioned response patterns. For example, in certain religious ceremonies, a person may report hearing voices, which is not considered abnormal by members of that religion, and the voices generally do not persist beyond the termination of such ceremonies.
Mood disorders	*Major depressive disorder*
	Symptoms of depression can be influenced by cultural and ethnic variables. For example, in certain cultures, symptoms of depression might be presented in somatic terms rather than as sadness or guilt. Among Latino and Mediterranean cultures, depressive experiences might be manifested in terms of complaints of "nerves" and headaches; Asians may show similar experiences in terms of weakness, tiredness, or "imbalance"; and among people from the Middle East and American Indian tribes, these experiences might be shown in terms of difficulties with the "heart" or being" heartbroken," respectively. The severity of the depression might also be evaluated differently across cultures (e.g., sadness may lead to less concern than irritability in some cultures). Actual hallucinations and delusions that are sometimes part of a major depressive disorder should be differentiated from cultural hallucinations and delusions (e.g., fear of being hexed and feeling of being visited by those who have died).

(continued)

disorder (Table 10.3). In other cases, *DSM-IV* did not provide a general statement of cultural variations covering a given disorder, but specific cultural considerations were given across subtypes within the disorder. For

(text continued on p. 132)

TABLE 10.1 *Continued*

Disorder	*Subtype*
Anxiety disorders	*Social phobia*
	In some cultures, social demands may lead to symptoms of social phobia. In certain cultures (e.g., Japan and Korea), an individual may develop persistent and excessive fears of giving offense to others in social situations instead of being embarrassed. These fears may be expressed in terms of extreme anxiety resulting from the belief that one's body odor, facial expression, or eye contact will be offensive to others (a culture-bound syndrome known as *taijin kyofusho*; see *DSM-IV,* 1994, p. 849; see also Chapter 9).
	Posttraumatic stress disorder (PTSD)
	Immigrants from countries with a high frequency of social unrest, wars, and civil conflicts may show high rates of PTSD. These immigrants may be particularly reluctant to divulge experiences of torture and trauma because of their political immigrant status.
Somatoform disorders	*Somaticization disorder*
	The frequency and type of somatic symptoms may vary across cultures. For example, people from Africa and South Asia tend to show more symptoms of burning hands and feet as well as nondelusional experiences of worms in the head or ants crawling under the skin in comparison to individuals from North America. In cultures in which semen loss is of great concern for their people, symptoms associated with male reproductive function tend to be more prevalent. In India, Sri Lanka, and China, severe anxiety associated with that concern is known as *dhat* (see *DSM-IV,* 1994, p. 846; see also Chapter 9).
Dissociative disorders	*Dissociative fugue*
	Some culture-bound syndromes may have symptoms resembling this disorder. For example, *pibloktoq* is a dissociative episode involving extreme excitement, convulsive seizures, and coma and is observed primarily in Arctic and subarctic Eskimo communities (see *DSM-IV,* 1994, p. 847; see also Chapter 9).
	Dissociative identity disorder
	It is suggested that this may be a culture-specific syndrome because the disorder tends to occur at a high rate in the United States.

TABLE 10.1 *Continued*

Disorder	Subtype
Eating disorders	*All subtypes*

All subtypes

Eating disorders are more prevalent in industrialized countries, including the United States, Canada, and Japan. In the case of anorexia nervosa, abundance of food and the linkage of attractiveness with being thin may explain the high rate of this disorder in such countries.

Impulse-control disorders not classified elsewhere

Intermittent explosive disorder

This disorder should be differentiated from the culturally bound syndrome known as *amok* (*DSM-IV*, 1994, p. 845; Chapter 9), which is characterized by an episode of acute, unrestrained violent behavior for which the individual claims amnesia. Amok is often reported among Southeast Asian countries, but cases have been reported in Canada and the United States. Amok often occurs as a single episode rather than as a pattern of aggressive behavior (more often seen among cases of intermittent explosive disorder) and is generally associated with prominent dissociative features.

Pathological gambling

Cultural variations have been reported in the prevalence and type of gambling activities, including cockfights and horse racing.

Personality disorders

Paranoid personality disorder

Behaviors influenced by sociocultural contexts or specific life circumstances may be erroneously labeled paranoid. For example, immigrants, political and economic refugees, and members of minority groups may show guarded or defensive behaviors because of either unfamiliarity with the language, rules, and regulations in the United States or the perceived neglect or indifference of the majority society.

Schizoid personality disorder

Defensive behaviors and interpersonal styles displayed by individuals from different cultural backgrounds may be erroneously considered as schizoid. For example, individuals who have moved from rural to metropolitan areas may show "emotional freezing" as manifested by solitary activities and constricted affect. Immigrants may also be mistakenly perceived as cold, hostile, and indifferent (additional suggested symptoms for this disorder).

(continued)

TABLE 10.1 *Continued*

Disorder	Subtype
Personality disorders (continued)	*Schizotypal personality disorder*
	Cognitive and perceptual distortions may be associated with religious beliefs and rituals, which may appear to be schizotypal to clinicians uninformed of these cultural variations. Examples of these distortions include voodoo ceremonies, speaking in tongues, belief in life beyond death, mind reading, evil eye, and magical beliefs associated with health and illness.
	Antisocial personality disorder
	Clinicians should consider the social and economic context in which the behaviors occur. Many behaviors associated with this disorder appear to be associated with low socioeconomic status, urban settings, and social contexts in which seemingly antisocial behaviors may be part of a protective survival strategy.

example, in the case of attention deficit and disruptive disorders, these variations were described for attention deficit/hyperactivity and conduct disorders; the subtype, oppositional defiant disorder, did not receive a discussion regarding these cultural variations. This explains why the name of a particular mental disorder (e.g., attention deficit and disruptive behavior disorders [ADDBD]) is repeated throughout Tables 10.1, 10.2, and 10.3 and its corresponding subtypes are listed in the appropriate table. For example, conduct disorder is listed in Table 10.1 because this subtype of ADDBD includes a description of cultural variations with examples; attention deficit/hyperactivity disorder is listed in Table 10.2 because this subtype of ADDBD includes a description of cultural variations without specific examples illustrating the applicability of these variations, and oppositional defiant disorder is included in Table 10.3 because this subtype of ADDBD does not include these variations and examples. Finally, several psychiatric diagnoses and their respective subtypes did not receive a description of cultural variations. These disorders are included in Table 10.3.

Cultural Considerations for Other Conditions
That May Be a Focus of Clinical Attention

The following five V codes (for Axis IV: Psychosocial and Environmental Problems) should be considered when using the cultural variations suggested by the *DSM-IV* (1994) and summarized in Tables 10.2 and 10.3:

TABLE 10.2 *DSM-IV* (1994) Disorders With Cultural Variations Without Examples

Disorder	*Subtype*
Mental retardation	*All subtypes*
	The individual's ethnic or cultural background should be taken into consideration during intellectual testing procedures. Use tests in which the person's relevant characteristics are represented in the standardization sample of the test or by employing an examiner familiar with aspects of the individual ethnic or cultural background.
Learning disorders	*All subtypes*
	Cultural variations are the same as described for mental retardation.
Communication disorders	*Expressive language disorder*
	The individual's cultural and language context must be taken into consideration during the assessment of the development of communication abilities, particularly for persons growing up in bilingual settings. The standardized measures of language development and of nonverbal intellectual capacity must be relevant for the cultural and linguistic group.
	Mixed receptive-expressive language disorder
	Same as above
	Phonological disorder
	Same as above
Attention deficit and disruptive behavior disorders	*Attention deficit/hyperactivity disorder*
	Is known to occur in various cultures, with variations in reported prevalence among Western countries as a result of different diagnostic practices rather than clinical presentation.
Feeding and eating disorders of infancy or early childhood	*Pica*
	Eating of dirt or other seemingly nonnutritive substances is considered of value in some cultures.
Tic disorders	*Tourette's disorder*
	This disorder is widely reported in diverse racial and ethnic groups.

(continued)

(text continues on p. 139)

TABLE 10.2 *Continued*

Disorder	*Subtype*
Other disorders of infancy, childhood, or adolescence	*Separation anxiety disorder*
	Clinicians should differentiate between separation anxiety disorder and the high value some cultures place on strong interdependence among family members. Cultural variations exist in the degree to which separation is tolerated.
	Selective mutism
	When immigrant children refuse to talk to strangers in a new environment because they are unfamiliar or uncomfortable with the new language, the diagnosis of selective mutism should not be used.
Amnestic disorder	*All subtypes*
	Educational and cultural variables should be considered in the assessment of memory. Persons from certain backgrounds might not be familiar with materials used in tests to assess memory.
Amphetamine-related disorders	*All subtypes*
	Dependence and abuse have been reported across all levels of society; intravenous use is more common among individuals from lower socioeconomic groups.
Cannabis-related disorders	*All subtypes*
	Cannabis is among the first drugs of experimentation for all cultural groups in the United States.
Cocaine-related disorders	*All subtypes*
	All race groups are affected by cocaine use. Its use by the most affluent has shifted to persons of low socioeconomic status living in metropolitan areas. Individuals from rural areas may also be affected.
Hallucinogen-related disorders	*All subtypes*
	Hallucinogens may be used as part of religious practices. Regional differences in their use have been reported in the United States.
Inhalant-related disorders	*All subtypes*
	Individuals living in economically depressed areas are particularly affected.
Nicotine-related disorders	*All subtypes*
	These disorders are decreasing in most industrialized countries and increasing in developing countries.

TABLE 10.2 *Continued*

Disorder	Subtype
Opioid-related disorders	*All subtypes*
	Opioid dependence among the white middle class in the earlier 1900s appears to have shifted toward minority groups living in economically depressed areas.
Phencyclidine-related disorders	*All subtypes*
	Prevalence appears to be higher among ethnic minorities (approximately twofold).
Sedative-hypnotic or anxiolytic-related disorders	*All subtypes*
	Marked variations in prescription patterns (and availability) of this class of substances are reported in different countries.
Schizophrenia and other psychotic disorders	*Delusional disorder*
	The individual's cultural and religious background should be considered in determining the possible presence of delusional disorder. The content of delusions varies across cultures.
Mood disorders	*Bipolar I disorder*
	A differential difference of bipolar I disorder on race or ethnicity has not been reported. Some evidence exists suggesting that clinicians may overdiagnose schizophrenia rather than bipolar disorder in some ethnic groups.
Anxiety disorders	*Panic disorder with or without agoraphobia*
	Panic attacks might include intense fear of magic or witchcraft in some cultures. Panic disorder as described in the *DSM-IV* (1994) has been reported in epidemiological studies throughout the world. In addition, several culturally bound syndromes described in the *DSM-IV* might be associated with panic disorder. The participation of women in public life is sometimes restricted in some ethnic and cultural groups, and this situation should be separated from agoraphobia.
	Specific phobia
	Both the content and the prevalence of this disorder vary with culture and ethnicity. Fears of magic or spirits are present in many cultures. These fears should be considered a specific phobia in cases in which the fear is excessive in the context of that culture and causes significant impairment and distress.

(continued)

TABLE 10.2 *Continued*

Disorder	Subtype
Anxiety disorders (continued)	*Obsessive-compulsive disorder* Behaviors that are culturally prescribed should be differentiated from obsessive-compulsive disorder, unless these culturally sanctioned behaviors exceed cultural norms, occur at times and places judged inappropriate by other members of the same culture, and interfere with social role functioning.
	Acute stress disorder The severity of this disorder may be determined by cultural differences in the implications of loss. Coping behaviors may also be culturally determined. For example, dissociative symptoms may be more common in cultures in which these symptoms are commonly accepted.
	Generalized anxiety disorder Considerable cultural variations exist in the expression of anxiety. In some cultures, anxiety is expressed predominantly through somatic symptoms, whereas in others, it is expressed through cognitive symptoms. The cultural context should be considered during the evaluation of whether worries about certain situations are excessive.
Somatoform disorders	*Undifferentiated somatoform disorder* Unexplained symptoms and worry about physical illness may be the result of culturally shaped "idioms of distress" used to express concerns about personal and social problems, without evidence of psychopathology.
	Conversion disorder This is reported to be more common in rural areas and among low-socioeconomic-status persons. Higher rates are reported in developing countries. Symptoms may reflect local cultural ideas about accepted and credible ways to express distress. Symptoms are common aspects of certain culturally sanctioned religious and healing rituals.
	Pain disorder Differences across cultural and ethnic groups exist in terms of how these groups react to pain and respond to painful stimuli.

TABLE 10.2 *Continued*

Disorder	Subtype
Somatoform disorders (continued)	*Hypochondriasis* Symptoms should be evaluated relative to the person's cultural background and explanatory models. Determine whether the individual's ideas about disease have been reinforced by traditional healers who may disagree with the reassurances given by medical evaluations. *Body dysmorphic disorder* Preoccupation with an imagined physical deformity may be determined by cultural concerns about physical appearance and the importance of physical self-presentation.
Dissociative disorders	*Depersonalization disorder* In many religions and cultures, induced experiences of depersonalization have been reported. These experiences should not be confused with depersonalization disorder.
Sexual dysfunctions	*All subtypes* The ethnic, cultural, and religious background of the individual should be considered during the assessment of sexual dysfunction. These cultural variations may affect sexual desire, expectations, and attitudes about performance. In some societies, female sexual desire is not considered very relevant, particularly when fertility is the primary concern.
Paraphilia	*All subtypes* What is considered appropriate in one culture may be viewed as inappropriate in other cultures; this makes the diagnosis of paraphilia across cultures and religions a complicated task for the clinician.
Parasomnias	*Nightmare disorder* The importance assigned to nightmares may vary with cultural background. In some cultures, nightmares are associated with spiritual or supernatural phenomena; in other cultures, nightmares may be viewed as indicators of mental or physical disturbances. *Sleep terror disorder* This disorder may differ across cultures, but clear evidence regarding culturally related differences in the presentation of this disorder is lacking.

(continued)

TABLE 10.2 *Continued*

Disorder	Subtype
Parasomnias (continued)	*Sleepwalking disorder* Same as above
Sleep disorders related to another mental disorder	*All subtypes* Sleep complaints may be viewed as less stigmatizing in some cultures than mental disorders. For this reason, individuals from some cultures may be more likely to show complaints of insomnia or hypersomnia rather than complaints involving symptoms of mental disorders such as depression and anxiety.
Impulse-control disorder not elsewhere classified	*Trichotillomania* It is more common in females than in males. This might reflect the gender ratio of the condition, or it might indicate the effect of cultural attitudes with respect to appearance (e.g., males' acceptance of normative hair loss).
Adjustment disorders	*All subtypes* The person's cultural setting should be considered to determine whether the individual's response to the stressor is either inappropriate or in excess of what would be expected in his or her culture. Variability exists across cultures with respect to the nature, meaning, experience of the stressor, and the evaluation of the response to the stressor.
Personality disorders	*Borderline personality disorder* Behaviors associated with this disorder have been seen in many settings around the world. *Histrionic personality disorder* Norms for personal appearance, emotional expressiveness, and interpersonal behavior vary widely across cultures. Symptoms associated with this disorder (e.g., emotionality, seductiveness, and impressionability) may be culturally accepted by the community; it is important to determine whether these symptoms cause clinically significant impairment or distress to the individual in comparison to what is culturally expected.

TABLE 10.2 *Continued*

Disorder	Subtype
Personality disorders (continued)	*Avoidant personality disorder*

Avoidant personality disorder

Variations exist in the degree to which different cultures and ethnic groups regard diffidence and avoidance as appropriate. Symptoms of this disorder may also result from acculturation problems associated with immigration.

Dependent personality disorder

The appropriateness of dependent behaviors varies among sociocultural groups. Behaviors associated with this disorder (e.g., passivity and difficulty in making everyday decisions) would be considered characteristic of this disorder only when they are clearly in excess of the individual's cultural norms or reflect unrealistic concerns. In addition, some cultures may differentially foster and discourage dependent behavior in males and females.

Obsessive-compulsive personality disorder

Habits, customs, or interpersonal styles culturally sanctioned by the individual's reference groups should not be included when making this diagnosis. The individual may place heavy emphasis on work and being productive because these behaviors are reinforced by the individual's reference group.

1. Partner Relational Problem (V61.1, p. 681)
2. Noncompliance With Treatment (V15.81, p. 683)
3. Religious or Spiritual Problem (V62.89, p. 685)
4. Acculturation Problem (V62.4, p. 685)
5. Parent-Child Relational Problem (V61.20, p. 681)

Partner Relational Problem

As noted earlier, cultural variables such as differences in the level of acculturation and the role of machismo and marianismo among Hispanic clients could lead to partner relational problems. For example, a Hispanic

TABLE 10.3 *DSM-IV* (1994) Disorders With Neither Cultural Variations
Nor Examples

Disorder	*Subtype*
Motor skills disorders	Developmental coordination disorder
Communication disorders	Stuttering
Pervasive developmental disorders	Autistic disorder, Rett's disorder, childhood disintegrative disorder, Asperger's disorder
Attention deficit and disruptive behavior disorders	Oppositional defiant disorder
Feeding and eating disorders of infancy or early childhood	Rumination disorder, feeding disorder of infancy or early childhood
Tic disorders	Chronic motor or vocal tic disorder, transient tic disorder
Elimination disorders	Encopresis, enuresis
Other disorders of infancy, childhood, or adolescence	Reactive attachment disorder of infancy or early childhood, stereotypic movement disorder
Mental disorders due to general medical condition	Catatonic disorder due to a general medical condition, personality change due to a general medical condition
Polysubstance-related disorders	All subtypes
Other (or unknown) substance-related disorders	All subtypes
Schizophrenia and other psychotic disorders	Shared psychotic disorder
Psychotic disorders due to general medical condition	Substance-induced psychotic disorder
Mood disorders	Dysthymic disorder, bipolar II disorder, cyclothymic disorder, other mood disorders
Mood disorders due to a general medical condition	Substance-induced mood disorder
Anxiety disorders	Anxiety disorder due to a general medical condition, substance-induced anxiety disorder
Factitious disorders	No subtype listed in *DSM-IV*
Dissociative disorders	Dissociative amnesia
Gender identity disorders	No subtype listed in *DSM-IV*
Sleep disorders	Primary insomnia, primary hypersomnia, narcolepsy, breathing-related sleep disorder, circadian rhythm sleep disorder
Other sleep disorders	Sleep disorder due to a general medical condition, substance-induced sleep disorder
Impulse-control disorders not elsewhere classified	Kleptomania, pyromania
Personality disorders	Narcissistic personality disorder

female may experience negative communications with her husband regarding their expectations of the role the wife should play at home if she does not share the values of machismo (men viewed as the authority in the family) and marianismo (women viewed as submissive, dependent, and obedient to the demands of the husband) often reinforced by many members of the Hispanic community. Similarly, an acculturated individual (e.g., someone who shares most values, lifestyle situations, and beliefs in the American culture) may have problems with a less acculturated partner who recently immigrated to the United States from a country with very distinct values, beliefs, and lifestyle situations. The example dealing with the impact of intertribal marriages on the discipline of the children (Chapter 6) also illustrates how cultural variables may lead to partner relational problems.

Noncompliance With Treatment

As noted in the *DSM-IV* (1994, p. 683), a client shows noncompliance with medical treatment because of his or her "personal values judgment or religious or cultural beliefs about the advantages and disadvantages of the proposed treatment." For example, American Indians believe that synthetic medication is not good for the health of Indians. Thus, an American Indian family may not follow through with the treatment involving a given drug for the management of a particular psychiatric disorder. As noted by Thompson, Walker, and Silk-Walker (1993), however, most classes of psychotropic mediation are effective in American Indian clients. The clinician's task is to accept those beliefs and values and then to gradually (through the psychotherapy process) introduce his or her views regarding the effectiveness of that drug (using empirical data) in the treatment of that particular disorder. Another example is the belief among many Asian clients that herbal medication can be used in combination with psychotropic medication in the treatment of physical and mental disorders. This combination may result in negative side effects, which a clinician should evaluate carefully (and inform the client). In this case, however, abruptly instructing an Asian client to stop using herbal medication may lead to noncompliance with the treatment.

Religious or Spiritual Problem

The *DSM-IV* (1994) suggests that a client's religious and spiritual beliefs may be the "focus of clinical attention" (p. 685) in those cases in which such a problem leads to "distressing experiences that involve loss or questioning of faith, problems associated with conversion to a new faith, or questioning of spiritual values" (p. 685). A religious or spiritual problem, however, may also be the focus of clinical attention in those cases in which a clinician believes that such a problem interferes with the overall assessment and treatment of the particular disorder. For example, many Hispanic clients believe that mental problems are caused by evil spirits, and, as a result, the church, not the clinician, has the power to treat these problems. Hispanics often believe that prayers will cure physical and mental problems, and help from a mental health professional is often sought when the family has exhausted all religious and folk resources to handle the problem. These religious and spiritual beliefs may directly or indirectly interfere with the assessment and treatment of a client.

Acculturation Problem

Clinicians should emphasize the process of acculturation as the "focus of clinical attention" when the problem involves "adjustment to a different culture (e.g., following migration)" (*DSM-IV,* 1994, p. 685). A discrepancy in the level or degree of acculturation among family members may be in itself the focus of clinical attention. This point was illustrated in Chapter 4 with the process of dating among Hispanic females. In this process, a Hispanic female is expected to engage immediate family members in that process (e.g., parents, uncles, brothers, and sisters). A highly acculturated Hispanic female residing with less acculturate family members may develop a psychiatric disorder (e.g., depression) because of this discrepancy in acculturation among members. In clinical practice, this discrepancy in acculturation levels should be the focus of clinical attention.

Acculturation scales provided in Table 8.1 may be used to determine whether or not an acculturation problem should be a focus of clinical attention during the management of given disorders in Axis I and Axis II in the *DSM-IV* (1994). In addition, clinicians are also encouraged to use the Brief Acculturation Scale suggested in Figure 2.1.

Parent-Child Relational Problem

A parent-child relational problem may include "impaired communication, overprotection, [and] inadequate discipline" (*DSM-IV,* 1994, p. 681). An acculturation problem may lead to a parent-child relational problem in the form of impaired communication. For example, later-generation Asian and Hispanic adolescents may disagree with their early-generation parents on certain issues involving customs and lifestyles (e.g., dressing and dating) because parents are less acculturated than their children into American society (see Chapter 4). The phenomenon of machismo among Hispanic fathers could lead to the overprotection of their children. Inadequate discipline of children and adolescents among American Indian parents may be the result of the parents belonging to different tribes (see Chapter 6). If a practitioner suspects that cultural variables can explain why these parent-child relational problems exist, these variables should be emphasized during the assessment and treatment of the particular family.

References

Allen, A. (1988). West Indians. In L. Comas-Díaz & E. E. H. Griffith (Eds.), *Clinical guidelines in cross-cultural mental health* (pp. 305-333). New York: John Wiley.

American Psychiatric Association. (1994). *Diagnostic and statistical manual of mental disorders* (4th ed.). Washington, DC: Author.

American Psychological Association. (1992). *Ethical principles of psychologists and code of conduct.* Washington, DC: Author.

Anastasi, A. (1988). *Psychological testing* (6th ed.). New York: Macmillan.

Anderson, L. P., Eaddy, C. L., & Williams, E. A. (1990). Psychosocial competence: Toward a theory of understanding positive mental health among Black Americans. In D. S. Ruiz & J. P. Comer (Eds.), *Handbook of mental health and mental disorder among Black Americans* (pp. 255-271). Westport, CT: Greenwood.

Anderson, W. H. (1988). The behavioral assessment of conduct disorder in Black children. In R. L. Jones (Ed.), *Psychoeducational assessment of minority group children: A case book* (pp. 103-123). Berkeley, CA: Cobb & Henry.

Arroyo, J. A. (1996). Psychotherapist bias with Hispanics: An analog study. *Hispanic Journal of Behavioral Sciences, 18,* 21-28.

Atkinson, D. R., & Wampold, B. E. (1993). Mexican Americans' initial preferences for counselors: Simple choice can be misleading—Comments on Lopez, Lopez, and Fong (1991). *Journal of Consulting Psychology, 40,* 245-248.

Baker, F. M. (1988). Afro-Americans. In L. Comas-Díaz & E. E. H. Griffith (Eds.), *Clinical guidelines in cross-cultural mental health* (pp. 151-181). New York: John Wiley.

Baker, F. M., & Lightfoot, O. B. (1993). Psychiatric care of ethnic elders. In A. C. Gaw (Ed.), *Culture, ethnicity, and mental illness* (pp. 517-552). Washington, DC: American Psychiatric Press.

Bamford, K. W. (1991). Bilingual issues in mental health assessment and treatment. *Hispanic Journal of Behavioral Sciences, 13,* 377-390.

145

Berg, I. K., & Jaya, A. (1993). Different and same: Family therapy with Asian-American families. *Journal of Marital and Family Therapy, 19,* 31-38.

Bernal, G., & Gutierrez, M. (1988). Cubans. In L. Comas-Díaz & E. E. H. Griffith (Eds.), *Clinical guidelines in cross-cultural mental health* (pp. 233-261). New York: John Wiley.

Berry, J. W., Poortinga, Y. H., Segall, M. H., & Darsen, P. R. (1992). *Cross-cultural psychology: Research and applications.* Cambridge, UK: Cambridge University Press.

Betancourt, H., & Lopez, S. R. (1993). The study of culture, ethnicity, and race in American psychology. *American Psychologist, 48,* 629-637.

Boucsein, W. (1992). *Electrodermal activity.* New York: Plenum.

Boyd-Franklin, N. (1989). *Black families, therapy: A multisystems approach.* New York: Guilford.

Brandon, W. (1989). *Indians.* Boston: Houghton Mifflin.

Bulhan, A. H. (1985). Black Americans and psychopathology: An overview of research and theory. *Psychotherapy, 22,* 370-378.

Burnam, M. A., Hough, R. L., Karno, M., Escobar, J. I., & Telles, C. A. (1987). Acculturation and lifetime prevalence of psychiatric disorders among Mexican Americans in Los Angeles. *Journal of Health and Social Behavior, 28,* 89-102.

Canino, I. A., & Canino, G. J. (1993). Psychiatric care of Puerto Ricans. In A. C. Gaw (Ed.), *Culture, ethnicity, and mental illness* (pp. 467-499). Washington, DC: American Psychiatric Press.

Cervantes, R. C., & Arroyo, W. (1994). DSM-IV: Implications for Hispanic children and adolescents. *Hispanic Journal of Behavioral Sciences, 16,* 8-27.

Choney, S. K., Berryhill-Paapke, E., & Robbins, R. R. (1995). The acculturation of American Indians: Developing frameworks for research and practice. In J. G. Ponterotto, J. M. Casas, L. A. Suzuki, & C. M. Alexander (Eds.), *Handbook of multicultural counseling* (pp. 73-92). Thousand Oaks, CA: Sage.

Chung, D. K. (1992). Asian cultural commonalities: A comparison with mainstream American culture. In S. M. Furuto, R. Biswas, D. K. Chung, K. Murase, & F. Ross-Sheriff (Eds.), *Social work practice with Asian Americans* (pp. 27-44). Newbury Park, CA: Sage.

Comas-Díaz, L. (1988). Cross-cultural mental health treatment. In L. Comas-Díaz & E. E. H. Griffith (Eds.), *Clinical guidelines in cross-cultural mental health* (pp. 337-361). New York: John Wiley.

Comas-Díaz, L., & Duncan, J. W. (1985). The cultural context: A factor in assertiveness training with mainland Puerto Rican women. *Psychology of Women Quarterly, 9,* 463-476.

Comas-Díaz, L., & Griffith, E. E. H. (Eds.). (1988). *Clinical guidelines in cross-cultural mental health.* New York: John Wiley.

Constantino, G., Malgady, R. G., & Rogler, L. H. (1988). *Technical manual: The TEMAS Thematic Apperception Test.* Los Angeles: Western Psychological Services.

Cook, K. O., & Timberlake, E. M. (1989). Cross-cultural counseling with Vietnamese refugees. In D. R. Koslow & E. P. Slett (Eds.), *Crossing cultures in mental health* (pp. 84-100). Washington, DC: International Counseling Center.

Costello, R. M., & Hays, J. R. (1988). *Texas law and the practice of psychology: A source book.* Austin: Texas Psychological Association.

Cuellar, I., Arnold, B., & Maldonado, R. (1995). Acculturation rating scale for Mexicans—II: A revision of the original ARSMA scale. *Hispanic Journal of Behavioral Sciences, 17,* 275-304.

Cuellar, I., Harris, L. C., & Jasso, R. (1980). An acculturation scale for Mexican American normal and clinical populations. *Hispanic Journal of Behavioral Sciences, 2,* 199-217.

Dana, R. H. (1993a, November 5). *Can "corrections" for culture using moderator variables contribute to cultural competence in assessment?* Paper presented at the annual convention of the Texas Psychological Association, Austin.

Dana, R. H. (1993b). *Multicultural assessment perspectives for professional psychology.* Boston: Allyn & Bacon.

Dana, R. H. (1995). Culturally competent MMPI assessment of Hispanic populations. *Hispanic Journal of Behavioral Sciences, 17,* 305-319.

De La Cancela, V. (1993). Rainbow warriors: Reducing institutional racism in mental health. *Journal of Mental Health Counseling, 15,* 55-71.

Dillard, J. L. (1973). *Black English: Its history and use in the United States.* New York: Vintage.

Escobar, J. E. (1993). Psychiatric epidemiology. In A. C. Gaw (Ed.), *Culture, ethnicity, and mental illness* (pp. 43-73). Washington, DC: American Psychiatric Press.

Eysenck, H. J., & Eysenck, S. B. S. (1975). *Manual for the Eysenck Personality Questionnaire.* San Diego: Educational and Industrial Testing Service.

Fairchild, H. H. (1985). Black, Negro, or African American? The differences are crucial. *Journal of Black Studies, 16,* 47-55.

Flaherty, J. A., Gaviria, M., Pathak, D., Mitchell, T., Wintrob, R., Richman, J. A., & Birz, S. (1988). Developing instruments for cross-cultural psychiatric research. *Journal of Nervous and Mental Disease, 176,* 257-263.

Flaskerud, J. H., & Anh, N. T. (1988). Mental health needs of Vietnamese refugees. *Hospital and Community Psychiatry, 39,* 435-436.

Fleming, C. M. (1992). American Indians and Alaska Natives: Changing societies past and present. In M. Orlandi & R. Weston (Eds.), *Cultural competence for evaluators* (pp. 147-171). Rockville, MD: U.S. Department of Health and Human Services.

Force, R. W., & Force, M. T. (1991). *The American Indians.* New York: Chelsea House.

Foreman, J. (1993, June 6). Navajos refuse to panic over perplexing disease. *Houston Chronicle,* pp. 1, 18.

Franco, J. N. (1983). An acculturation scale for Mexican American children. *Journal of General Psychology, 108,* 175-181.

French, L. A. (1993). Adapting projective tests for minority children. *Psychological Reports, 72,* 15-18.

Fujii, J. S., Fukushima, S. N., & Yamamoto, J. (1993). Psychiatric care of Japanese Americans. In A. C. Gaw (Ed.), *Culture, ethnicity, and mental illness* (pp. 305-345). Washington, DC: American Psychiatric Press.

Garcia, M., & Lega, L. I. (1979). Development of a Cuban ethnic identity questionnaire. *Hispanic Journal of the Behavioral Sciences, 1,* 247-261.

Garza-Treviño, E., Ruiz, P., & Venegas-Samuels, K. (1997). A psychiatric curriculum directed to the care of the Hispanic patient. *Academic Psychiatric, 21,* 1-10.

Gaw, A. C. (Ed.). (1993a). *Culture, ethnicity, and mental illness.* Washington, DC: American Psychiatric Press.

Gaw, A. C. (1993b). Psychiatric care of Chinese Americans. In A. C. Gaw (Ed.), *Culture, ethnicity,and mental illness* (pp. 245-280). Washington, DC: American Psychiatric Press.

Golden, C. J. (1990). *Clinical interpretation of objective psychological tests* (2nd ed.). Needham, MA: Allyn & Bacon.

Goodluck, C. T. (1993). Social services with Native Americans: Current status of the Indian Child Welfare Act. In H. P. McAdoo (Ed.), *Family ethnicity: Strength and diversity* (pp. 217-226). Newbury Park, CA: Sage.

Graham, J. R. (1990). *MMPI-2: Assessing personality and psychopathology.* New York: Oxford University Press.

Gregory, S. (1996). "We've been down this road already." In S. Gregory & R. Sanjek (Eds.), *Race* (pp. 18-38). New Brunswick, NJ: Rutgers University Press.

Grieger, I., & Ponterotto, J. G. (1995). A framework for assessment in multicultural counseling. In J. G. Ponterotto, J. M. Casas, L. A. Suzuki, & C. M. Alexander (Eds.), *Handbook of multicultural counseling* (pp. 357-374). Thousand Oaks, CA: Sage.

Griffith, E. E. H., & Baker, F. M. (1993). Psychiatric care of African Americans. In A. C. Gaw (Ed.), *Culture, ethnicity, and mental illness* (pp. 147-173). Washington, DC: American Psychiatric Press.

Griffith, E. E. H., English, T., & Mayfield, V. (1980). Possession, prayer, and testimony: Therapeutic aspects of the Wednesday night meeting in a Black church. *Psychiatry, 43,* 120-128.

Harjo, S. S. (1993). The American Indian experience. In H. P. McAdoo (Ed.), *Family ethnicity: Strength in diversity* (pp. 199-216). Newbury Park, CA: Sage.

Helms, J. E. (1986). Expanding racial identity theory to cover the counseling process. *Journal of Counseling Psychology, 33,* 62-64.

Helzer, J. E., Burnam, A., & McEvoy, L. T. (1991). Alcohol abuse and dependence. In L. N. Robins & D. A. Regier (Eds.), *Psychiatric disorders in America: The epidemiologic catchment area study* (pp. 81-115). New York: Free Press.

Ho, M. K. (1987). *Family therapy with ethnic minorities.* Newbury Park, CA: Sage.

Ho, M. K. (1992). *Minority children and adolescents in therapy.* Newbury Park, CA: Sage.

Hoffmann, T., Dana, R., & Bolton, B. (1985). Measured acculturation and MMPI-168 performance of Native American adults. *Journal of Cross-Cultural Psychology, 16,* 243-256.

Holtzman, W. H. (1988). Beyond the Rorschach. *Journal of Personality Assessment, 52,* 578-609.

Hughes, C. C. (1993). Culture in clinical psychiatry. In A. C. Gaw (Ed.), *Culture, ethnicity, and mental illness* (pp. 3-41). Washington, DC: American Psychiatric Press.

Ivey, A. E., Ivey, M. B., & Simek-Morgan, L. (Eds.). (1996). *Counseling and psychotherapy: A multicultural perspective.* Boston: Allyn & Bacon.

Jackson, A., Berkowitz, H., & Farley, G. (1974). Race as a variable affecting the treatment involvement of children. *Journal of the American Academy of Child Psychiatry, 13,* 20-31.

Jackson, E. L., & Westmoreland, G. (1992). Therapeutic issues for Black children in foster care. In L. A. Vargas & J. D. Koss-Chioino (Eds.), *Working with culture: Psychotherapeutic interventions with ethnic minority children and adolescents* (pp. 43-62). San Francisco: Jossey-Bass.

Jaimes, M. A. (1996). American racism: The impact on American-Indian identity and survival. In S. Gregory & R. Sanjek (Eds.), *Race* (pp. 41-61). New Brunswick, NJ: Rutgers University Press.

Jalali, B. (1988). Ethnicity, cultural adjustment, and behavior: Implications for family therapy. In L. Comas-Díaz & E. E. H. Griffith (Eds.), *Clinical guidelines in cross-cultural mental health* (pp. 9-32). New York: John Wiley.

Jenkins, J. O., & Ramsey, G. A. (1991). Minorities. In M. Hersen, A. E. Kazdin, & A. S. Bellack (Eds.), *The clinical psychology handbook* (pp. 724-740). New York: Pergamon.

Johnson, T. M., Fenton, B. J., Kracht, B. R., Weiner, M. F., & Guggenheim, F. G. (1988). Providing culturally sensitive care: Intervention by a consultation-liaison team. *Hospital and Community Psychiatry, 39,* 200-202.

Jones, A. C. (1992). Self-esteem and identity in psychotherapy with adolescents from upwardly mobile middle-class African American families. In L. A. Vargas & J. D. Koss-Chioino (Eds.), *Working with culture: Psychotherapeutic interventions with ethnic minority children and adolescents* (pp. 25-42). San Francisco: Jossey-Bass.

Joyce, P. R., & Paykel, E. S. (1989). Predictors of drug response in depression. *Archives of General Psychiatry, 46,* 89-99.

Karkabi, B. (1993, July 21). More than semantics: Heritage, image influence Blacks' self-perception. *Houston Chronicle,* pp. 1D, 5D.

Karno, M., & Golding, J. M. (1991). Obsessive compulsive disorder. In L. N. Robins & D. A. Regier (Eds.), *Psychiatric disorders in America* (pp. 204-219). New York: Free Press.

Kaufman, S., Kamphaus, R. W., & Kaufman, N. L. (1985). New directions in intelligence testing: The Kaufman Assessment Battery for Children (K-ABC). In B. B. Wolman (Ed.), *Handbook of intelligence: Theories, measurements, and applications* (pp. 663-698). New York: John Wiley.

Keith, S. J., Regier, D. A., & Rae, D. S. (1991). Schizophrenic disorders. In L. N. Robins & D. A. Regier (Eds.), *Psychiatric disorders in America: The Epidemiologic Catchment Area Study* (pp. 33-52). New York: Free Press.

Kilkus, M. D., Pumariega, A. J., & Cuffe, S. P. (1995). Influence of race on diagnosis in adolescent psychiatric inpatients. *Journal of the American Academy of Child and Adolescent Psychiatry, 34,* 67-72.

Kim, L. I. C. (1993). Psychiatric care of Korean Americans. In A. C. Gaw (Ed.), *Culture, ethnicity, and mental illness* (pp. 347-375). Washington, DC: American Psychiatric Press.

Kim, S., McLeod, J. H., & Shantzis, C. (1992). Cultural competence for evaluators working with Asian-American communities: Some practical considerations. In M. Orlandi & R. Weston (Eds.), *Cultural competence for evaluators* (pp. 203-260). Rockville, MD: U.S. Department of Health and Human Services.

Kim, S. C. (1985). Family therapy for Asian Americans: Strategic-structural framework. *Psychotherapy, 22,* 342-348.

Kinzie, J. D., & Leung, P. K. (1993). Psychiatric care of Indochinese Americans. In A. C. Gaw (Ed.), *Culture, ethnicity, and mental illness* (pp. 281-304). Washington, DC: American Psychiatric Press.

Kolko, D. J. (1987). Simplified inpatient treatment of nocturnal enuresis in psychiatrically disturbed children. *Behavior Therapy, 2,* 99-112.

Koslow, D. R., & Slett, E. P. (Eds.). (1989). *Crossing cultures in mental health.* Washington, DC: International Counseling Center.

Koslow, N. J., & Rehm, L. P. (1991). Childhood depression. In T. R. Kratochwill & R. J. Morris (Eds.), *The practice of child therapy* (2nd ed., pp. 43-75). New York: Pergamon.

Kratochwill, T. R., & Bergan, J. R. (1990). *Behavioral consultation in applied settings: An individual guide.* New York: Plenum.

LaFromboise, T. D., Foster, S., & James, A. (1996). Ethics in multicultural counseling. In P. B. Pedersen, J. G. Draguns, W. J. Lonner, & J. E. Trimble (Eds.), *Counseling across cultures* (pp. 47-72). Thousand Oaks, CA: Sage.

Lange, A. J., & Jakubowski, P. (1976). *Responsible assertive behavior.* Champaign, IL: Research Press.

Leaf, P. J., Myers, J. K., & McEvoy, L. T. (1991). Procedures used in the Epidemiologic Catchment Area Study. In L. N. Robins & D. A. Regier (Eds.), *Psychiatric disorders in America: The epidemiologic Catchment Area Study* (pp. 11-30). New York: Free Press.

Lefley, P., & Pedersen, P. B. (Eds.). (1986). *Cross-cultural training for mental health professionals.* Springfield, IL: Charles C Thomas.

Levin, J. S., & Taylor, R. J. (1993). Gender and age differences in religiosity among Black Americans. *The Gerontologist, 33,* 16-23.

Lineberger, M. H., & Calhound, K. S. (1983). Assertive behavior in Black and White American undergraduates. *Journal of Psychology, 13,* 139-148.

Lonner, W. J., & Ibrahim, F. A. (1996). Appraisal and assessment in cross-cultural counseling. In P. B. Pedersen, J. G. Draguns, W. J. Lonner, & J. E. Trimble (Eds.), *Counseling across cultures* (pp. 293-322). Thousand Oaks, CA: Sage.

Lopez, S., & Nunez, J. A. (1987). Cultural factors considered in selected diagnostic criteria and interview schedule. *Journal of Abnormal Psychology, 96,* 270-272.

Lopez, S. R., Lopez, A. A., & Fong, K. T. (1991). Mexican Americans' initial preferences for counselors: The role of ethnic factors. *Journal of Counseling Psychology, 38,* 487-496.

Malgady, R. G., Constantino, G., & Rogler, L. H. (1984). Development of a thematic apperception test (TEMAS) for urban Hispanic children. *Journal of Consulting and Clinical Psychology, 52,* 986-996.

Malgady, R. G., Rogler, L. H., & Constantino, G. (1987). Ethnocultural and linguistic bias in mental health evaluation of Hispanics. *American Psychologist, 42,* 228-234.

Manson, S. M., Walker, R. D., & Kivlahan, D. R. (1987). Psychiatric assessment and treatment of American Indians and Alaska Natives. *Hospital Community Psychiatry, 38,* 165-173.

Marcos, L. R. (1976). Bilinguals in psychotherapy: Language as an emotional barrier. *American Journal of Psychotherapy, 30,* 552-560.

Marcos, L. R., Alpert, M., Urcuyo, L., & Kesselman, M. (1973). The effect of interview language on the evaluation of psychopathology in Spanish-American schizophrenic patients. *American Journal of Psychiatry, 130,* 549-553.

Marin, G., & Marin, B. V. (1991). *Research with Hispanic populations.* Newbury Park, CA: Sage.

Martinez, C. (1986). Hispanic psychiatric issues. In C. Wilkinson (Ed.), *Ethnic psychiatry* (pp. 61-87). New York: Plenum.

Martinez, C. (1988). Mexican-Americans. In L. Comas-Díaz & E. E. H. Griffith (Eds.), *Clinical guidelines in cross-cultural mental health* (pp. 182-203). New York: John Wiley.

Martinez, C. (1993). Psychiatric care of Mexican Americans. In A. C. Gaw (Ed.), *Culture, ethnicity, and mental illness* (pp. 431-466). Washington, DC: American Psychiatric Press.

Martinez, R. E. (1993, August). Minority label "dehumanizing" [Letter to the editor]. *San Antonio Express News,* p. 5B.

Masuda, M., Matsumoto, G. H., & Meredith, G. M. (1970). Ethnic identity in three generations of Japanese Americans. *Journal of Social Psychology, 81,* 199-207.

Matheson, L. (1986). If you are not an Indian, how do you treat an Indian? In H. P. Lefley & P. B. Pedersen (Eds.), *Cross-cultural training for mental health professionals* (pp. 115-130). Springfield, IL: Charles C Thomas.

McAdoo, H. P. (1993a). Ethnic families: Strengths that are found in diversity. In H. P. McAdoo (Ed.), *Family ethnicity: Strength in diversity* (pp. 3-14). Newbury Park, CA: Sage.

McAdoo, H. P. (Ed.). (1993b). *Family ethnicity: Strength in diversity.* Newbury Park, CA: Sage.

Mendoza, R. H. (1989). An empirical scale to measure type and degree of acculturation in Mexican-American adolescents and adults. *Journal of Cross-Cultural Psychology, 20,* 372-385.

Mercer, J., & Lewis, J. (1978). *System of multicultural pluralistic assessment.* New York: Psychological Corporation.

Milliones, J. (1980). Construction of a Black consciousness measure: Psychotherapeutic implications. *Psychotherapy: Theory, Research, and Practice, 17,* 175-182.

Moffic, H. S., & Kinzie, J. D. (1996). The history and future of cross-cultural psychiatric services. *Community Mental Health Journal, 32,* 581-592.

Mollica, R. F. (1989). Developing effective mental health policies and services for traumatized refugee patients. In D. R. Koslow & E. P. Slett (Eds.), *Crossing cultures in mental health* (pp. 101-115). Washington, DC: International Counseling Center.

Mollica, R. F., & Lavelle, J. (1988). Southeast Asian refugees. In L. Comas-Díaz & E. E. H. Griffith (Eds.), *Clinical guidelines in cross-cultural mental health* (pp. 262-293). New York: John Wiley.

Montgomery, G. T., & Orozco, S. (1985). Mexican Americans' performance on the MMPI as a function of level of acculturation. *Journal of Clinical Psychology, 41,* 203-212.

Moyerman, D. R., & Forman, B. D. (1992). Acculturation and adjustment: A meta-analytic study. *Hispanic Journal of Behavioral Sciences, 14,* 163-200.

Mueller, J., Kiernan, R. J., & Langston, J. W. (1992). The mental status examination. In H. H. Goldman (Ed.), *Review of general psychiatry* (pp. 109-117). San Mateo, CA: Appleton & Lange.

Murase, K. (1992). Models of service delivery in Asian American communities. In S. M. Furuto, R. Biswas, D. K. Chung, K. Murase, & F. Ross-Sheriff (Eds.), *Social work practice with Asian Americans* (pp. 101-119). Newbury Park, CA: Sage.

Musser-Granski, J., & Carrillo, D. F. (1997). The use of bilingual, bicultural professionals in mental health services: Issues for hiring, training, and supervision. *Community Mental Health Journal, 33,* 51-60.

Neff, J. A., & Hoppe, S. K. (1993). Race/ethnicity, acculturation, and psychological distress: Fatalism and religiosity as cultural resources. *Journal of Community Psychology, 21,* 3-20.

Neighbors, H. W., & Lumpskin, S. (1990). The epidemiology of mental disorder in Black population. In D. S. Ruiz (Ed.), *Handbook of mental health and mental disorder among Black Americans* (pp. 55-70). Westport, CT: Greenwood.

Norris, A. E., Ford, K., & Bova, C. A. (1996). Psychometrics of a brief acculturation scale for Hispanics in a probability sample of urban Hispanic adolescents and young adults. *Hispanic Journal of Behavioral Sciences, 18,* 29-38.

O'Brien, S. (1989). *American Indian tribal governments.* Norman: University of Oklahoma Press.

Paniagua, F. A. (1996). Cross-cultural guidelines in family therapy practice. *Family Journal: Counseling and Therapy for Couples and Families, 4,* 127-138.

Paniagua, F. A., & Baer, D. M. (1981). A procedural analysis of the symbolic forms of behavior therapy. *Behaviorism, 9,* 171-205.

Paniagua, F. A., & Black, S. A. (1990). Management and prevention of hyperactivity and conduct disorders in 8-10 year old boys through correspondence training procedures. *Child and Family Behavior Therapy, 12,* 23-56.

Paniagua, F. A., O'Boyle, M., Tan, V. L., & Lew, A. S. (1998). *Self-evaluation of biases and prejudices.* Manuscript submitted for publication.

Paniagua, F. A., Wassef, A., O'Boyle, M., Linares, S. A., & Cuellar, I. (1993). What is a difficult mental health case? An empirical study of relationships among domain variables. *Journal of Contemporary Psychotherapy, 23,* 77-98.

Pedersen, P. (1987). *Handbook of cross-cultural counseling and therapy.* London: Greenwood.

Pedersen, P. B. (1997). *Culture-centered counseling interventions: Striving for accuracy.* Thousand Oaks, CA: Sage.

Pedersen, P. B., Draguns, J. G., Lonner, W. J., & Trimble, J. E. (Eds.). (1996). *Counseling across cultures.* Thousand Oaks, CA: Sage.

Phinney, J. S. (1996). When we talk about American ethnic groups, what do we mean? *American Psychologist, 51,* 918-927.

Pierce, R. C., Clark, M., & Kiefer, C. W. (1972). A "bootstrap" scaling technique. *Human Organization, 31,* 403-410.

Pitta, P., Marcos, L. R., & Alpert, M. (1978). Language switch as a treatment strategy with bilingual patients. *American Journal of Psychoanalysis, 38,* 255-258.

Ponterotto, J. G., Casas, J. M., Suzuki, L. A., & Alexander, C. M. (Eds.). (1995). *Handbook of multicultural counseling.* Thousand Oaks, CA: Sage.

Pope-Davis, D. B., & Coleman, H. L. K. (Eds.). (1997). *Multicultural counseling competencies: Assessment, education and training, and supervision.* Thousand Oaks, CA: Sage.

Pumariega, A. J., Nace, D., England, M. J., Diamond, J., Mattson, A., Fallon, T., Hanson, G., Lourie, I., Marx, L., Thurber, D., Winters, N., Graham, M., & Wiegand, D. (1997). Community-based systems approach to children's managed mental health services. *Journal of Child and Family Studies, 6,* 149-164.

Radloff, L. S. (1977). The CES-D scale: A self-report depression scale for research in the general public. *Applied Psychological Measurement, 1,* 385-401.

Ramirez, M. (1984). Assessing and understanding biculturalism-multiculturalism in Mexican-American adults. In J. L. Martinez & R. H. Mendoza (Eds.), *Chicano psychology* (pp. 77-94). Orlando, FL: Academic Press.

Ramirez, S. Z., Paniagua, F. A., Linskey, A., & O'Boyle, M. (1993, August). *Diagnosing mental disorders in Hispanic children and youth: Cultural considerations.* Paper presented at the annual convention of the American Psychological Association, Toronto, Canada.

Ramirez, S. Z., Wassef, A., Paniagua, F. A., & Linskey, A. O. (1993, November). *The significance of cultural evaluations of psychopathology in ethnic minority individuals.* Paper presented at the annual convention of the Texas Psychological Association, Austin.

Ramirez, S. Z., Wassef, A., Paniagua, F. A., Linskey, A. O., & O'Boyle, M. (1994). Perceptions of mental health providers concerning cultural factors in the evaluation of Hispanic children and adolescents. *Hispanic Journal of Behavioral Sciences, 16,* 28-42.

Ramos-McKay, J. M., Comas-Díaz, L., & Rivera, L. A. (1988). Puerto Ricans. In L. Comas-Díaz & E. E. H. Griffith (Eds.), *Clinical guidelines in cross-cultural mental health* (pp. 204-232). New York: John Wiley.

Reyhner, J., & Eder, J. (1988). A history of Indian education. In J. Reyhner (Ed.), *Teaching American Indian students* (2nd ed., pp. 33-58). Norman: University of Oklahoma Press.

Richardson, E. H. (1981). Cultural and historical perspectives in counseling American Indians. In D. W. Sue (Ed.), *Counseling the culturally different: Theory and practice* (pp. 216-255). New York: John Wiley.

Robins, L. R., Helzer, J. F., Weissman, M. M., Orvasche, H., Gruenberg, E., Burke, J. D., & Regier, D. A. (1984). Lifetime prevalence of specific psychiatric disorders in three sites. *Archives of General Psychiatry, 41,* 949-958.

Robins, L. R., & Regier, D. A. (1991). *Psychiatric disorders in America: The Epidemiologic Catchment Area Study.* New York: Free Press.

Rogler, L. H. (1993). Culture in psychiatric diagnosis: An issue of scientific accuracy. *Psychiatry, 56,* 324-327.

Root, M., Ho, C., & Sue, S. (1986). Issues in the training of counselors for Asian Americans. In H. P. Lefley & P. B. Pedersen (Eds.), *Cross-cultural training for mental health professionals* (pp. 199-209). Springfield, IL: Charles C Thomas.

Rubel, A. J., O'Nell, C. W., & Collado-Ardon, R. (1984). *Susto: A folk illness.* Berkeley: University of California Press.

Ruiz, R. A. (1981). Cultural and historical perspectives in counseling Hispanics. In D. W. Sue (Ed.), *Counseling the culturally different: Theory and practice* (pp. 186-215). New York: John Wiley.

Ruiz, R. A., & Padilla, A. M. (1977). Counseling Latinos. *Personnel and Guidance Journal, 55,* 401-408.

Russell, D. M. (1988). Language and psychotherapy: The influence of nonstandard English in clinical practice. In L. Comas-Díaz & E. E. H. Griffith (Eds.), *Clinical guidelines in cross-cultural mental health* (pp. 33-68). New York: John Wiley.

Russo, N. F., Olmedo, E. L., Stapp, J., & Fulcher, R. (1981). Women and minorities in psychology. *American Psychologist, 36,* 1315-1363.

Rutter, M., Tuma, A. H., & Lann, I. S. (1988). *Assessment and diagnosis in child psychopathology.* New York: Guilford.

Sandoval, M. C., & De La Roza, M. C. (1986). A cultural perspective for serving Hispanic clients. In H. P. Lefley & P. B. Pedersen (Eds.), *Cross-cultural training for mental health professionals* (pp. 151-181). Springfield, IL: Charles C Thomas.

Seijo, R., Gomez, H., & Freidenberg, J. (1991). Language as a communication barrier in medical care for Hispanic patients. *Hispanic Journal of Behavioral Sciences, 13,* 363-376.

Silver, B., Poland, R. E., & Lin, K. (1993). Ethnicity and the pharmacology of tricyclic antidepressants. In K. Lin, R. E. Poland, & G. Nakasaki (Eds.), *Psychopharmacology and psychobiology of ethnicity* (pp. 61-89). Washington, DC: American Psychiatric Press.

Simons, R. C., & Hughes, C. C. (1993). Cultural-bound syndromes. In A. C. Gaw (Ed.), *Culture, ethnicity, and mental illness* (pp. 75-93). Washington, DC: American Psychiatric Press.

Smith, E. J. (1981). Cultural and historical perspectives in counseling Blacks. In D. W. Sue (Ed.), *Counseling the culturally different: Theory and practice* (pp. 141-185). New York: John Wiley.

Smith, T. W. (1992). Changing racial labels: From "colored" to "Negro" to "Black" to "African American. " *Public Opinion Quarterly, 56,* 496-544.

Smither, R., & Rodriguez-Giegling, M. (1982). Personality, demographics, and acculturation of Vietnamese and Nicaraguan refugees to the United States. *International Journal of Psychology, 17,* 19-25.

Smitherman, G. (1995). *Black talk.* Boston: Houghton Mifflin.

Soto, E. (1983). Sex-role traditionalism and assertiveness in Puerto Rican women living in the United States. *Journal of Community Psychology, 11,* 346-354.

Spitzer, R. L., & Endicott, J. (1978). *The schedule for affective disorders and schizophrenia* (3rd ed.). New York: New York State Psychiatric Institute.

Sue, D., & Sundberg, N. D. (1996). Research and research hypotheses about effectiveness in intercultural counseling. In P. B. Pedersen, J. G. Draguns, W. J. Lonner, & J. E. Trimble (Eds.), *Counseling across cultures* (pp. 323-352). Thousand Oaks, CA: Sage.

Sue, D. W., & Sue, D. (1987). Asian-Americans and Pacific Islanders. In P. Pedersen (Ed.), *Handbook of cross-cultural counseling and therapy* (pp. 141-146). London: Greenwood.

Sue, D. W., & Sue, D. (1990). *Counseling the culturally different: Theory and practice* (2nd ed.). New York: John Wiley.

Sue, S. (1988). Psychotherapy services for ethnic minorities: Two decades of research findings. *American Psychologist, 43,* 301-308.

Sue, S., Fujino, D. C., Hu, L., Takeuchi, D. T., & Zane, N. W. S. (1991). Community mental health services for ethnic minority groups: A test of the cultural responsiveness hypothesis. *Journal of Consulting and Clinical Psychology, 59,* 433-540.

Sue, S., & Zane, N. (1987). The role of culture and cultural techniques in psychotherapy. *American Psychologist, 42,* 37-45.

Suinn, R. M., Rickard-Figueroa, K., Lew, S., & Vigil, S. (1987). The Suinn-Lew Asian Self-Identity Acculturation scale: An initial report. *Educational and Psychological Measurement, 47,* 401-407.

Szapocznik, J., Scopetta, M. A., Arnalde, M., & Kurtines, W. (1978). Cuban value structure: Treatment implications. *Journal of Consulting and Clinical Psychology, 46,* 961-970.

Tanaka-Matsumi, J., & Higginbotham, H. N. (1996). Behavioral approaches to counseling across cultures. In P. B. Pedersen, J. G. Draguns, W. J. Lonner, & J. E. Trimble (Eds.), *Counseling across cultures* (pp. 266-292). Thousand Oaks, CA: Sage.

Taylor, R. J., & Chatters, L. M. (1986). Church-based informal support among elderly blacks. *The Gerontologist, 26,* 637-642.

Tharp, R. G. (1991). Cultural diversity and treatment of children. *Journal of Consulting and Clinical Psychology, 59,* 799-812.

Thompson, J., Walker, R. D., & Silk-Walker, P. (1993). Psychiatric care of American Indians and Alaska Natives. In A. C. Gaw (Ed.), *Culture, ethnicity, and mental illness* (pp. 189-243). Washington, DC: American Psychiatric Press.

Trimble, J. E., & Fleming, C. M. (1989). Providing counseling services for Native American Indians: Client, counselor, and community characteristics. In P. B. Pedersen, J. G. Draguns, W. J. Lonner, & J. E. Trimble (Eds.), *Counseling across cultures* (3rd ed., pp. 177-204). Honolulu: University of Hawaii Press.

Tsui, A. M. (1985). Psychotherapeutic considerations in sexual counseling for Asian immigrants. *Psychotherapy, 22,* 357-362.

U.S. Bureau of the Census. (1996). *Statistical abstract for the United States.* Washington, DC: Government Printing Office.

U.S. Department of Health and Human Services. (1991). *Health status of minorities and low-income groups: Third edition.* Washington, DC: Health Resources and Services Administration, U.S. Department of Health and Human Services.

Walker, R. D., & LaDue, R. (1986). An integrative approach to American Indian mental health. In C. B. Wilkinson (Ed.), *Ethnic psychiatry* (pp. 143-199). New York: Plenum.

Westermeyer, J. J. (1993). Cross-cultural psychiatric assessment. In A. C. Gaw (Ed.), *Culture, ethnicity, and mental illness* (pp. 125-144). Washington, DC: American Psychiatric Press.

Wilkinson, C. B. (1986). Introduction. In C. B. Wilkinson (Ed.), *Ethnic psychiatry* (pp. 1-11). New York: Plenum.

Wilkinson, C. B., & Spurlock, J. (1986). The mental health of Black Americans: Psychiatric diagnosis and treatment. In C. B. Wilkinson (Ed.), *Ethnic psychiatry* (pp. 13-59). New York: Plenum.

Wilkinson, D. (1993). Family ethnicity in America. In H. P. McAdoo (Ed.), *Family ethnicity: Strength in diversity* (pp. 15-59). Newbury Park, CA: Sage.

Wise, F., & Miller, N. B. (1983). The mental health of American Indian children. In G. J. Powell, J. Yamamoto, A. Romero, & A. Morales (Eds.), *The psychosocial development of minority group children* (pp. 344-361). New York: Brunner/Mazel.

Wolpe, J., & Lang, P. J. (1964). A fear survey schedule for use in behavior therapy. *Behaviour Research and Therapy, 2,* 27-30.

Wong-Rieger, D., & Quintana, D. (1987). Comparative acculturation of Southeast Asians and Hispanic immigrants and sojourners. *Journal of Cross-Cultural Psychology, 18,* 145-162.

Yamamoto, J. (1986). Therapy for Asian Americans and Pacific Islanders. In C. B. Wilkinson (Ed.), *Ethnic psychiatry* (pp. 89-141). New York: Plenum.

Yamamoto, J., Silva, J. A., Justice, L. R., Chang, C. Y., & Leong, G. B. (1993). Cross-cultural psychotherapy. In A. C. Gaw (Ed.), *Culture, ethnicity, and mental illness* (pp. 101-124). Washington, DC: American Psychiatric Press.

Subject Index

Acculturation:
  African Americans and, 27-28,101
  American Indians and, 11
  Asians and, 71,72
  assessment of, 105
  defined, 8
  ethnicity and, 5
  external, 9-10
  Hispanics and, 10, 45, 46-47, 50, 51, 52
  internal, 9-10
  interpretation of clinical data and,
    100-101
  interpretation of psychological data and,
    100-101
  levels of, 10-12
  psychiatric epidemiological data and,
    100-101
Acculturation Balance Scale, 102
Acculturation Questionnaire, 102
Acculturation Rating Scale for Mexican
    Americans, 101,102
African Americans:
  church affiliation and, 22, 28-29
  Black English and, 3 24-25, 99
  Bible study groups and, 23

cultural paranoia and, 23, 37
depression and, 30
discussion of racial differences and, 25-27
empowerment and, 34
familism and, 21-22
family secrets and, 31-32
folk beliefs and.
folk medicine and, 23
grandmother and, 29-30
healthy paranoid and, 23
income and, 20
internal acculturation and, 27
level of acculturation and, 27-28
modalities of therapy and, 34-47
poverty and, 20
problem-solving training and, 34-35
racial labels and, 20-21
religious beliefs and, 22
role flexibility and, 21-22
schizophrenia and, 30-31
standard American English and, 24-25
street talk and, 24-25
strengths of, 32-33
substance abuse and, 30-31
voodoo priests and, 23

About the Author

Freddy A. Paniagua, Ph.D. (University of Kansas; postdoctoral training at Johns Hopkins University School of Medicine), is Professor in the Department of Psychiatry and Behavioral Sciences, University of Texas Medical Branch at Galveston, where he teaches cross-cultural mental health seminars with an emphasis on the assessment and treatment of African American, Hispanic, Asian, and American Indian clients. In 1989, he received a 6-year training grant from the National Institute of Mental Health to provide postdoctoral and postmaster training to mental health professionals representing different multicultural groups with emphasis on the assessment and treatment of emotionally disturbed clients. He has published more than 35 scientific articles, including basic and applied research and theoretical contributions.